CREATIVE HOMEOWNER®

AFFORDABLE
BATHROOM
Upgrades

CRE▲TIVE
HOMEOWNER®

AFFORDABLE

BATHROOM

Upgrades

Transform Your Bathroom on a Small Budget

Steve Cory
and
Diane Slavik

CREATIVE HOMEOWNER®, Upper Saddle River, New Jersey

AFFORDABLE BATHROOM UPGRADES

AUTHORS	Steve Cory, Diane Slavik
TECHNICAL ADVISERS	Joe Hansa, Bill West
GRAPHIC DESIGNERS	Glee Barre, Scott Kraft
DIGITAL IMAGING SPECIALISTS	Fred Becker, Segundo Gutierrez
INDEXER	Sandi Schroeder, Schroeder Indexing Services

Manufactured in the United States of America

Current Printing (last digit)
10 9 8 7 6 5 4 3

Affordable Bathrooms Upgrades
Library of Congress Control Number: 2011939710
ISBN-10: 1-58011-557-8
ISBN-13: 978-1-58011-557-5

CREATIVE HOMEOWNER®
A Division of Federal Marketing Corp.
24 Park Way
Upper Saddle River, NJ 07458
www.creativehomeowner.com

Safety

Although the methods in this book have been reviewed for safety, it is not possible to overstate the importance of using the safest methods you can. What follows are reminders—some do's and don'ts of work safety—to use along with your common sense.

- Always use caution, care, and good judgment when following the procedures described in this book.
- Always be sure that the electrical setup is safe, that no circuit is overloaded, and that all power tools and outlets are properly grounded. Do not use power tools in wet locations.
- Always read container labels on paints, solvents, and other products; provide ventilation; and observe all other warnings.
- Always read the manufacturer's instructions for using a tool, especially the warnings.
- Use hold-downs and push sticks whenever possible when working on a table saw. Avoid working short pieces if you can.
- Always remove the key from any drill chuck (portable or press) before starting the drill.
- Always pay deliberate attention to how a tool works so that you can avoid being injured.
- Always know the limitations of your tools. Do not try to force them to do what they were not designed to do.
- Always make sure that any adjustment is locked before proceeding. For example, always check the rip fence on a table saw or the bevel adjustment on a portable saw before starting to work.
- Always clamp small pieces to a bench or other work surface when using a power tool.
- Always wear the appropriate rubber gloves or work gloves when handling chemicals, moving or stacking lumber, working with concrete, or doing heavy construction.
- Always wear a disposable face mask when you create dust by sawing or sanding. Use a special filtering respirator when working with toxic substances and solvents.
- Always wear eye protection, especially when using power tools or striking metal on metal or concrete; a chip can fly off, for example, when chiseling concrete.
- Never work while wearing loose clothing, open cuffs, or jewelry; tie back long hair.

- Always be aware that there is seldom enough time for your body's reflexes to save you from injury from a power tool in a dangerous situation; everything happens too fast. Be alert!
- Always keep your hands away from the business ends of blades, cutters, and bits.
- Always hold a circular saw firmly, usually with both hands.
- Always use a drill with an auxiliary handle to control the torque when using large-size bits.
- Always check your local building codes when planning new construction. The codes are intended to protect public safety and should be observed to the letter.
- Never work with power tools when you are tired or when under the influence of alcohol or drugs.
- Never cut tiny pieces of wood or pipe using a power saw. When you need a small piece, saw it from a securely clamped longer piece.
- Never change a saw blade or a drill or router bit unless the power cord is unplugged. Do not depend on the switch being off. You might accidentally hit it.
- Never work in insufficient lighting.
- Never work with dull tools. Have them sharpened, or learn how to sharpen them yourself.
- Never use a power tool on a workpiece—large or small—that is not firmly supported.
- Never saw a workpiece that spans a large distance between horses without close support on each side of the cut; the piece can bend, closing on and jamming the blade, causing saw kickback.
- When sawing, never support a workpiece from underneath with your leg or other part of your body.
- Never carry sharp or pointed tools, such as utility knives, awls, or chisels, in your pocket. If you want to carry any of these tools, use a special-purpose tool belt that has leather pockets and holders.

Contents

Introduction

Do you want to change the look or usability of your bathroom but don't have tens of thousands of dollars for a remodel? This is the book for you. The following pages show many ways to make substantial improvements—not just redecorating—without spending a lot of money and with minimal disruption to daily routines.

You could say that the projects in this book are mid-level improvements. We won't talk about nuclear-option remodeling—tearing out walls or opening floors to move drainpipes, or moving the tub, sink, or toilet to a new location. But we'll go way beyond painting the walls or putting up a couple of towel racks (though both of those are worthy projects). You'll be able to make the most of the layout you have, and you won't have to settle for less than what you want.

Unless your bathroom is a total disaster area, chances are that you can transform yours into something you love by executing four or five of our projects. As long as you're willing to roll up your sleeves and do the work yourself, most of the projects will cost less than $300, and very few of them will cost more than $1,500 (unless you buy, say, a $1,600 faucet). The instructions in the book will guide you surely along the way. If you hire someone to do the work, you may need to double those prices. That's still far less than a remodel will cost. And in most cases you won't lose the use of your bathroom for more than a day or two.

Redoing a bathroom one step at a time calls for concentration and work that is sometimes hard, but it can also be fun. Work with family members, or at least consult with them during the planning stages. Spend plenty of time choosing just the right materials; shopping can often take more time than installation, but it's usually time well spent. Work methodically and carefully, even if it means an extra hour or even day. Once you're finished, you will feel proud of your accomplishment and pleased with the results of your labor.

All of the elements in this bathroom, left—tiled tub surround, tub and shower controls, custom shower curtain, vanity with sink and faucet, sconce lights, tile floor, and even the tub itself—are inexpensive features that you can install, usually in less than a day. This book shows how to do them all.

A few very modest but well-thought-out changes can make a big difference in a bathroom, opposite. A quick-install shelf, towel rack, and blow-dryer hook, as well as a rug and towels that coordinate with the wall tiles, make the room feel upscale—an outsized reward for such a small outlay in money and labor.

1
Upgrade Possibilities

Bathroom remodeling can be an expensive proposition, but there are dozens of improvements that cost relatively little. Often two or three modest changes can dramatically change the appearance and usefulness of a bathroom, for instance:

- If the tub and toilet look OK, installing new flooring (which shouldn't cost much because a bathroom is typically small) and an easy-to install vanity with sink top will add visual punch, create storage space, and make the floor easier to clean.

- Painting walls, installing new window treatments, and replacing towel racks, hooks, and hardware are inexpensive projects that can make a bathroom look totally new.

- Cleaning the tub-and-shower tiles and grout and installing a new showerhead, spout, and faucet handles typically takes a couple hours and can make a dingy shower surround gleam.

- Replacing an old toilet and lavatory with new fixtures that will modernize and harmonize a bathroom, and both projects can be easily accomplished over a weekend.

Clean and Light

A major reason for renovating a bathroom is that after years of use and abuse, it loses the clean feeling that makes it inviting. Real estate experts that say a spotless bathroom is critical to avoid a negative reaction from prospective home buyers. Predominantly white or light-colored bathrooms have an enduring appeal because they look so clean and healthy, and that, after all, corresponds with the purpose of the bathroom. If you're leaning toward a white or whitish color scheme, you'll probably be mixing and matching shades and textures. For instance, your sink and toilet may be pure shiny white, and your walls and other surfaces may be different shades of white and textures. For turn-of-the-century appeal, consider subway tiles for the walls and small hexagonal tiles for the floor.

If you've ever looked at white and off-white paints at a paint store, you know how wide the array of shades is. Color experts say the key to coordinating whites is to choose shades from the same family: either yellow-based or blue-based. Using colors from different families can result in an overall gray or dingy effect.

However, mixing textures will add depth to the overall design, and surfaces that are textured or tumbled (as well as painted woodwork such as bead-board) nicely complement nearby smooth and shiny surfaces. Glass surfaces such as glass block or glass shower doors further enhance the overall beauty of the white palette.

For accents, choose colors that are again in the same family as your whites—either blue or yellow. As an accent color, use straight blue, bluish green, bluish yellow, or purple. For yellow accents, colors can include yellow-green (shades of olive) or yellow-red (shades of orange). Accents can be big or small, so you might want just occasional splashes of color, or you might want to make a larger surface, such as a countertop or tub surround, a contrasting color.

The neat gray-and-white palette in this bathroom, below left, has a neutral masculine flavor that offers a lot of design flexibility. The whole ambiance will quickly evolve by adding accents like a colorful rug, shower curtain, hanging picture, or even towels.

Natural light from a nearby window adds a dreamy overlay to light blue walls and a wood-toned floor, below right. Narrow horizontal accent tiles in the tub surround play off the wall color and picture frames. Coordinated details—faucet, racks, and paper holder—unify the room and add dignity.

The bathroom opposite is nearly bipolar: the bottom half is all white tiles and fixtures, while the upper half features natural woodwork and a wall faux-painted with earth tones. The clean, earthy combination is very inviting.

Soothing Minimalism

In recent years, the style pendulum has swung toward an appreciation for a more simple and basic design in the bathroom—an approach that cuts the clutter and lets the clean shine through so that when you walk into the room, you feel a sense of serenity and pleasure. Unlike the cold "Euro style" of the 80s and 90s, which featured hard surfaces and stainless steel, today's minimalist decor is perfect for a bathroom that is used for relaxing and unwinding.

To achieve this effect, the bathroom's overall design will have clean lines, understated furnishings, and soft lighting. The color scheme is generally calm, muted, and neutral—for instance, shades of white, beige, or gray. Candles are a popular accent, and spare quantities of weather-worn shelving and furnishings add warmth and elegance to complete the look.

This style works best for people who can keep things neat and tidy. If you have children or have a difficult time keeping things in order, it may help to provide storage space nearby, perhaps in a hall closet.

The clean geometric emphasis in this bathroom, above, together with the crisp contrast of its three colors, brings old-fashioned elements to life with striking clarity.

Clean lines and a serene color scheme, below, provide a warm backdrop for a bathroom that features an inexpensive acrylic tub and a simple toilet and sink.

Wide planks of reclaimed flooring on the wall, above, echo the wide lines of the tiling on the floor. The subdued earthy shades of gray and tan in the room's surfaces establish a rustic tone that pleasantly contrasts with the pure white color and graceful lines of the sink and toilet.

The farm-style wall-hung sink, right, sets the tone in this bathroom. An unornamented recessed medicine cabinet hides storage space within the wall cavity, and a simple glass shelf provides just a bit of storage. Only a few colorful and textured accents are needed to complete the mood of this bright and inviting room.

Mix and Match

With a small room like a bathroom, it's easy to choose a theme and run with it. An eclectic style tends to mix things up a bit and be more of a unique expression of individual taste. The result is a room that's a little surprising and a lot of fun.

If you make one change at a time, perhaps as budget permits, you'll be better able to tinker with the design as you go along. If you look at photos of designer bathrooms, you may notice that they are not as neatly coordinated as they used to be; instead, designers are mixing up styles and colors to make the overall design more interesting. As you gradually develop an overall design for your bathroom, let your creative impulses and personal preferences guide you to include colors and styles that you like; you can tie the room together with textiles, baskets, or well-chosen lighting.

A giant mirror, along with nooks cut into walls, seems to enlarge this modest-size kids' bathroom, top right. Unusual color choices reinforce the "fun" childlike theme.

Victorian playfulness in the bathroom above is achieved with a curvy pink sink set into a curve-cut granite vanity top. Over-the-top mirrors and accessories complete the picture.

The glass block window in this bathroom, right, disperses crazy splashes of light over the wallpaper and tiles. The polished brass faucet glinting in the light adds a ritzy splash.

A shell collection is the theme of this luxury bathroom, right, where glittering wall surfaces elevate the design, contrasting with the black cabinetry. The pebble-based flooring resembles a beach, and all of the accents reinforce the theme.

In this funky bathroom, below, walls are partially covered with salvaged barn boards; the flooring is made of extra-wide knotty pine planks, and a new pale green utility sink looks like a refinished antique.

Furniture and Fabrics

It used to be that bathrooms had their own special style of furniture—vanities, medicine chests, and over-the-toilet shelving units that you wouldn't see elsewhere in the house. But times have changed. Many of today's bathroom furnishings are more dignified: antique furniture and accent pieces that might be at home in your living room lend warmth and make the bathroom more inviting as a place to lounge and unwind.

Area rugs that you might find in other rooms of the house are becoming more common in bathrooms as well. Designers say better-quality rugs will actually absorb less water than cheaper rugs, though of course you'll still want a bath mat to catch most of the water.

For lighting, consider a floor lamp (plugged into a ground-fault circuit-interrupter receptacle) and other lights that you might find in a living room—track or recessed lights, for instance. If you have architectural details like crown molding, consider positioning fluorescent lights to emphasize them—in a cove or under a soffit, for instance.

Baskets, tiles, and textiles help tie the room together and make it a one-of-a-kind retreat.

Stand-alone furniture, left, can serve as a room divider as well as valuable storage space.

A Victorian swag shower curtain, top, gracefully frames this elegant bathtub nook.

This section of the bathroom, above, doesn't look like a bathroom at all; the highboy and upholstery fabric under the sink would work well in a living room. The unobtrusive wall-mounted faucet over the bowl sink and the antique accents complete the look.

Some bathroom vanities are now made in a distinctly furniture style. The drain for this unit snakes out of view to allow ample room for storage below. (See pages 56-57.)

Cottage Style

Today, as many people have a more relaxed and casual approach to decorating, the cottage style has enduring appeal. It used to be that a family's summer cottage by the sea was furnished with cast-offs from the nicer city home—old china, worn furniture, and the like—for a charming mismatched effect. In this spirit, scavenged items are a good resource to consider, especially items that have an appealing level of imperfections. A coat of paint can help tie mismatched pieces together. Bead board for walls, ceilings, or cabinet doors helps establish a cottage feel, even if some of your big-ticket items, such as a tub and toilet, are a little more modern. Cottage decorating has evolved in recent years, so you can buy projects that look pleasantly shabby. The result can produce a range of overall effects—maybe feminine, maybe rustic, maybe neat and prim.

Most vanities have a single door. This vanity, above, has a bottom drawer—a simple change that makes a stunning difference and adds a cozy feel. It also greatly enhances the usable storage space.

The feminine bathroom opposite features a simple board-and-batten wall that is painted pale pink. The vanity leaves the drain plumbing exposed, allowing for an open shelf and a drawer with a fluted front.

In this bathroom, right, the same bead board is repeated on the wainscot, the vanity, and the tub apron. Marble tub-surround tiles make the cottage theme more elegant. A shelf just wide enough for knickknacks caps the bead-board wainscot.

This powder room, below, was covered with uninspired sheet paneling, but covering it with a coat of happy-looking paint spiced it up quickly. Blue and green, spa colors, are a splashy and refreshing twist on the cottage style.

Most of the storage items, above, are on display in this light and bright bathroom. Shelves that resemble wrought iron have old-style appeal and keep creature comforts within easy reach.

Color Decisions

We've all been told at some point that neutral colors are the best choice in a home, and many people are afraid to depart from conservative color themes. But adding color in the bathroom is an easy and inexpensive way to dramatically change the look and feel of the room.

The Bold

Two high-contrast colors—or a bold color abutting a bright whitish color—will have a crisp, vibrant effect. Walking into a bathroom, it's surprising to see bold colors because we tend to expect traditional white. If your bathroom has some imperfections, bold colors can draw the eye away and emphasize the overall design in the room so that the imperfections recede visually. Tiles are commonly used around a tub or shower, but a wall or stripe of tiles, perhaps in a vivid color, placed on other walls can add pizzazz.

Because this powder room is small, above, the lavish tile installation is not as expensive as you might expect. The dominant dark colors work well because of the visual variety in the design, and the room does not appear smaller. Dividing the room in half horizontally lends a dressy effect, like a white shirt and dark pants.

This elegant bathroom, left, owes a lot of its charm to the paint job. Simple pieces of white railing, which can easily be added to walls, help accentuate the Victorian design and the contrast between the two colors. The ornate mirror adds a Louis XV touch, but otherwise the room's furnishings are not expensive.

Sea blue tiles that seem to roll along the wall makes this bathroom shimmer, above. Whether a judicious thin stripe or an entire wall, the glitter of mosaics can have a magical effect.

Hot accent colors, right, perk up a somewhat somber palette of the walls and floor. Mosaics on one wall add texture and interest, while the dark gold color on the other wall helps tie the interesting color scheme together.

Orange and green walls in this bathroom, left, are certainly visually arresting. The yellow sink top and blue chair add to the eclectic feel. Dark wood-toned floor and vanity-wall treatments provide neutral spaces between the colors that make the effect cheerful rather than jarring.

Soft blue-gray plays off the blue-tinged white tub surround tiles, above. Coming from the opposite end of the color spectrum, yellow accents liven up the design.

Natural earth tones, including the color of the tub and toilet, below, create an unusual bathroom palette, but the harmony of the colors and textures is warm, inviting, and dignified.

The Subdued

For a more soothing, mellow effect, choose different intensities or values of the same color—two shades of pale blue, for instance. Using different shades of the same color can add depth and balance and can help highlight the better features of the room. Color experts say that contrary to popular belief, painting a small room a deep color does not necessarily make it seem smaller. The trick is to use different values of the color—and to add texture. Then the overall design is more interesting, which makes the eyes move around and the room seem bigger.

The soft, muted colors in this bathroom, above, more typical of a living room, seem to glow from the warmth of the sconces on each side of the mirror. Sparing accent color contributes to a minimalist feel.

The Fun

The colors you choose set the mood for the room. Cool colors such as blue or green work well in a bathroom, perhaps because they evoke the feeling of a spa, a welcome retreat. Yellow is definitely staging a comeback these days—somehow it can seem subdued and vibrant at the same time.

Glass tiles in a checkerboard pattern, left, run halfway up the wall to spice up the design in this attic bathroom.

A simple tile pattern like this one, above, adds creative flair to a bathroom's design. A narrow horizontal stripe of the same (or another) pattern would also be an interesting effect.

Consider Yellow

Various shades of yellow have an almost magical ability to brighten and sooth your spirit. When lit by the morning sun, yellow tones provide a needed pick-me-up; in the evening, yellow walls and fabrics attain a mellow state, as if candlelit.

Enhanced Accessibility

According to a recent survey by the American Association of Retired Persons, nearly 90 percent of older adults say they would like to stay in their current residence as long as possible. In response, bathroom manufacturers are creating a variety of products to make that goal easier to attain. If you need to accommodate a wheelchair, your bathroom may need more extensive renovations than this book offers—widening a doorway or knocking out a wall, for instance. However, if your needs are not that drastic, there are a number of easy-to-install products that can make your bathroom safer and easier to navigate.

Accessibility does not need to look industrial. This shower area, right, has a tiled niche and a wooden seat that is as lovely as it is comfortable.

A step-in bathtub like this one, below, is easier to get in and out of.

To install a grab bar like this by the toilet, below, you would need to add plywood or 2-by lumber reinforcement inside the bathroom wall.

A higher toilet, bottom, can make getting up and down less of a chore. You could simply install a raised toilet seat, but a special toilet like this is more stable and substantial-looking, and will cost you about $200 and a few hours labor.

A wall-hung sink (page 50) has space underneath to accommodate a wheelchair. This drop-in sink, mounted onto a shelf with no legs (top), accomplishes the same thing.

Faucet handles like these, above, are easier to manipulate, especially for older adults with arthritis.

Old-Fashioned Appeal

A bathroom design that reflects the decorating genius of an earlier decade, perhaps the pink tiles that were common in the 50s, the olive green of the 60s or orange of the 70s, or the classy art deco style of the 20s, can be a charming theme for a bathroom. Today's manufacturers have created a wealth of high-performance products in beautiful vintage style.

To achieve this effect, start by choosing your room's big-ticket items first, aiming for a pleasant symmetry, then move on to the other details. With such a small room, it's easier to achieve a unified effect that will echo the era you're after, and because it's a small room, you need only a few well-chosen details, like the mirror, the lighting, or a retro clock, to help define the look and tie the room together.

If you have a favorite traditional style—say, Victorian or Mission—it can be fun to research the accessories, furnishings, and color themes of the era to achieve an authentic effect, perhaps by visiting a historical society or museum. Newer homes often lack the ornamental effects of bygone eras, and adding details like wood molding, baseboard, or a ceiling medallion can help define the look. To complement wood details, consider other natural materials, like stone and tile. Stone commonly used a century ago included marble, slate, or soapstone, but not the glossy granite that is so popular today.

Salvaged building materials are a good resource for a vintage bathroom. For instance, if you can find reclaimed wood, especially wider-plank flooring, you can use it for flooring or wall panels. Other details might include a stained-glass window perhaps salvaged from an old church to hang in your bathroom window, an antique piece of furniture for a vanity or bathroom storage, and decorative touches like art glass or an old mirror or frame. Replicas of antique lighting, like sconces, can complete the look.

This bathroom, above, features Italian-style tiles with complementary accent bands; ensembles like this are widely available today. The pedestal sink, toilet, and black metal racks, shelves, and fixtures look old-fashioned but are new replicas.

Olive or avocado green was a favorite color of the 70s, left, and you can capture the cachet of that decade just by choosing floor or wall tiles in the appropriate shade. You may need to peruse the Internet to find a toilet seat of just the right color.

This vanity, below, is topped with a vessel sink that resembles an old-fashioned washbowl. The racks, towel hook, and faucet are finished to look like weathered metal.

In this rustic bathroom, bottom, salvaged drawers and shelves are reminiscent of an old farmhouse; covering them with satin sealer makes them resistant to water damage and easy to clean.

A number of venerable features, above, such as molding frames on the lower wall, "dentil" trim that travels around the wall and mirror, vertically striped wallpaper, and sumptuous drapery, give this bathroom great character.

You can get old-fashioned appeal, below, by combining several inexpensive components: a "console" sink with elegant legs, small white tiles with even smaller black diamond accents, painted wainscoting, a mirror with faux-painted frame, and striped wallpaper.

Kid Stuff

Kids grow up quickly, so a little flexibility in the design of a children's bath is a good idea. Your daughter may love pink when she's four, but when she's eight or nine, she may be passionate about blue. In that case, a new coat of paint or a new shower curtain is much easier to update than a tiled tub surround. However, even grown-ups enjoy the occasional whimsical tile dotting the bathroom landscape. Stencils and removable decals are another possibility for bathroom tiles or walls, and it can be fun to change them every year or two.

Stenciled fish, above, seem to swim off the walls in this playful and colorful bathroom.

Frog stencils, below right, seem to leap out of nowhere in this bold bathroom color scheme that features the sort of bright contrasts that children enjoy. Removable wall decals are another option for design flexibility.

You need not sacrifice adult tastes to make a bathroom kid friendly. This bathroom, above, has only a few easily removed decorative touches that make it inviting to a youngster.

Storage Options

Bathroom storage makes a big contribution to the style of the room. If you're tired of the traditional vanity for under-sink storage, consider open shelves with baskets or a skirted sink. Where you have open wall space, floating shelves and hooks or rails keep things in the open for a fun casual look.

This console sink, left, features two drawers and a nice open shelf—which amounts to more usable space than a standard vanity.

This casual but modern-feeling bathroom, above, is fitted with inexpensive shelves and cabinets that are available at home and department stores. Often these stores will provide a variety of sizes and shapes that can be tailored to fit your space.

Creative solutions for towel racks and shelves are fun to incorporate into bathroom design. A stool and ladder, right, conveniently positioned, serve as a shelf and towel rack, respectively.

Divine Details

The fun thing about remodeling a bathroom is how noticeable small changes are. Even something as minor as changing out towel racks or adding a slender row of tiles above the sink will make the room more visually interesting and enjoyable. Upgrading lighting or adding a shelf or railing for storage are opportunities to add color and dress up the feel of the room.

A decorative band of glass and rope-trim tiles, above, makes all the difference between plain and *Wow!* and is well worth the modest extra cost.

This metal shelf over the towel rack, below, takes advantage of space near the ceiling that otherwise might not be used. An artfully positioned matching robe hook helps accentuate the quality of the metal details.

The walls in this bathroom, above, have a memorable stone look created by combining flat stones with rough plaster—a job for pros. The sink, with its distinctive rounded edges, is a nice complement to the classic antique-style cabinet serving as a vanity.

This medicine cabinet, left, is recessed into the wall for good shelf depth without protruding into the room. The curved cut glass with beveled edge is a distinctive design that's a cut above the usual plain rectangle. Wall sconce lights with a gleaming chrome sheen match the cabinet frame.

This lovely faucet, bottom left, is just right: quietly elegant without being gaudy or pretentious—substantial with a slightly retro look. Choose your faucet carefully, and don't hesitate to spend a bit more for one you love.

A small slab of granite resting on top of an old furniture piece, below, is the starting point for this bathroom's decor. The tiles, mirror, sconce, ceramic self-rimming sink, and faucet are well-chosen details that together have a richly textured appeal.

2

Faucets, Sinks, and Toilets

The workhorses of the bathroom, faucets, sinks, and toilets get used many thousands of times a year. Fortunately, most reasonably priced units made by well-known manufacturers will perform their tasks reliably; only bargain-bin fixtures made by off-brand companies are likely to give you trouble. That means you can base your shopping decisions primarily on finding the features and styles that please you. This chapter will guide you in making decisions and installing units. In most cases, a motivated homeowner with a modest set of tools can replace an existing sink, faucet, or toilet with another one in the same location. If you want to add another unit or move a plumbing fixture to another part of the bathroom, it is probably best to call in a professional plumber.

Choosing Faucets

A standard traditional bathroom faucet fits onto a bathroom lavatory sink with three holes (the outer holes being 4 inches apart from center to center) and may operate with one or two handles. Nowadays, however, a growing number of one-handle faucets are made to go into one hole only. If you are installing a vessel sink, also called a bowl sink, with no faucet holes, you will have to install the faucet in the countertop or the wall.

Most faucets come with a pop-up assembly, which includes a flange (the part you see at the drain hole), a drain body (also called a tailpiece) that screws up into the flange under the sink, and the linkage parts that move the stopper up and down to seal or open the drain.

Some faucets, especially wall-mounted types and those used with vessel sinks, do not have a pop-up assembly, however, and instead rely on a drain body with a hand-operated stopper.

Make sure the faucet has a spout that delivers water at a point that is comfortable to reach and fairly near the center of the bowl.

Choose a faucet with a finish that matches or harmonizes with other features in the bathroom, such as the tub and shower handles and spout. Chrome is durable and inexpensive, but you can enhance the look of a bathroom with fixtures made of materials like stainless steel, brushed nickel, or bronze (which itself comes in several hues). A PVD (physical vapor deposition) has the appearance of polished brass but never tarnishes and is easy to clean.

If you want your faucet to come out of the wall, opposite, you'll need to run pipes inside the wall and have them emerge at just the right points. See pages 46–47 for steps on installing supply plumbing.

As long as you're drilling holes in a countertop for a faucet, you may choose to add a feature like a soap dispenser, above left.

If the sink does not have faucet-mounting holes, above right, you can install the faucet into a hole bored in the cabinet. Be sure the faucet is tall enough to gracefully deliver water into the sink.

A tall bowl sink, right, requires an extra-tall faucet. In most cases, a single-handle model is the easiest to use.

Sinks Galore

In the past decade or two, bathroom sinks, also called lavatories or lavs, have become available in a wide variety of styles, colors, materials, and even shapes. Vessel, or bowl, lavatories have become especially popular in recent years.

How Will the Plumbing Look? *TIP*

If you have an inexpensive (but actually very durable) plastic drain trap as well as less-than-attractive stop valves and supply tubes, installing a vanity cabinet will cover them and hide the ugliness. Depending on how the plumbing is positioned in the wall, the plumbing may be left open to view if you install a wall-hung, pedestal, console, or other type of sink. See page 49 for tips on installing more-attractive sink plumbing. If you need to move the plumbing in the wall to reposition the stop valves, see pages 220–225.

A wall-mounted sink, left, attaches to the wall, leaving the plumbing underneath exposed. Old-fashioned plain wall-mounted sinks have gone out of favor, but newer types are making a comeback, some of which incorporate towel racks. If you need a bathroom to be accessible for a person in a wheelchair, a wall-mounted sink is the best choice.

A vanity, below, is made of a cabinet (usually wood) with a sink that rests on top. The sink is typically a one-piece molded (also called integral) top that includes some counter space as well as the bowl. A vanity is easy to install and provides useful storage space below. A molded top is easy to clean because there are no crevices or edges around the bowl.

A pedestal sink, opposite, is much like a wall-hung sink, but it rests on a central pedestal. Many pedestal sinks have a retro or Victorian look, but modern styles are also available. A pedestal sink is a bit impractical because it provides no storage cabinetry and limits the baskets you can place under it.

A drop-in sink (also called a self-rimming sink) fits onto a hole cut in a vanity (or console) top, opposite. The top may be made of granite, other stone, or laminate materials, or it may be covered with custom tiles, as shown on pages 68–71. If the sink comes in for heavy use, you'll spend a bit of extra time cleaning around the sink's edges. Oval, shallow-rimmed sinks are traditional and still the most common, but today drop-in sinks are made in rectangular and other shapes, and some have rims thick enough to make them similar in appearance to a bowl sink.

Hybrid Sinks

Some newer styles blur the distinction between vanity, pedestal and wall-hung sinks. Options include metal pedestals that may be purely decorative or may provide shelving; wood cabinets with open shelves rather than doors; and sinks supported by two porcelain legs rather than a central pedestal.

Also called vessel sinks, bowl sinks, left, rest on top of a cabinet countertop. The faucet may attach to the sink but more often comes out of the countertop or the wall. Vessel sinks are made of a wide variety of materials, including glass, ceramic, metal, stone, china, and even bamboo.

An under-mount sink, below, behaves much like a molded (integral) sink but is composed of a sink bowl mounted to the underside of a countertop. The top is typically made of granite, marble, or other polished stone. The sink's hole must have polished edges because they are exposed. It's not practical for a homeowner to make up an under-mount sink; instead, purchase one that is already cut and polished.

Bathroom Faucet

Installing a new bathroom faucet is not a difficult job, especially because today's faucets have a gasket that seals the baseplate to the sink. Most bathroom faucets, like the one shown here, include a drain body/ tailpiece and a pop-up assembly for raising and lowering the drain stopper. Buy braided supply tubes that are long enough to reach from the faucet to your stop valves in the wall, and make sure they have the right-sized fittings to match your stop valves (which may be either ½ inch or ⅜ inch).

A two-handle faucet typically is installed onto a sink or counter-top with three holes. This chrome faucet's handles are gracefully curved, like the spout.

Basin Wrench for Tight Spots

If you are installing a faucet onto a sink that is not in place, installation is very easy. If the sink is already installed, however, you will have to crawl below with a flashlight and use a basin wrench (as shown) to reach the parts.

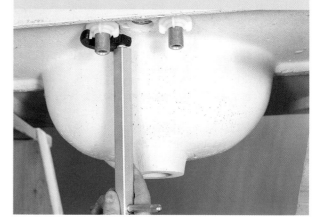

Connecting the Pop-Up

First you'll need to install the combination drain body/ tailpiece pipe. Slip the pivot rod in ❶; tighten the nut; and connect the pop-up linkage ❷. See pages 62-63 for more instructions.

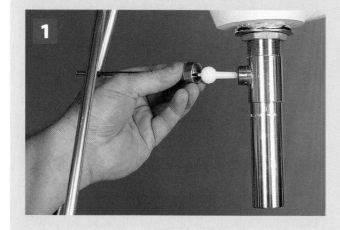

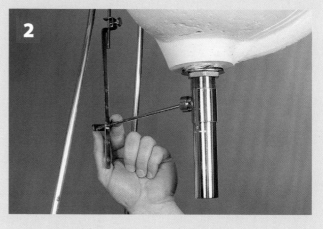

Replacing a Bathroom Faucet

• Putty knife • Groove-point pliers • Basin wrench • Bathroom sink with pop-up assembly • Plumber's putty

1 Shut off the stop valves, and test to make sure water is off. Set a small bucket under the valve, and disconnect the supply tubes. Disconnect the mounting hardware, and remove the old faucet. Use a putty knife, then a sponge and degreaser, to clean the sink deck.

2 Position the gasket on the sink, or snap it in place onto the underside of the faucet. Slip the faucet's supply inlets through the holes in the sink.

3 Some faucets mount using nuts that thread onto the faucet's inlets. (See page 63.) Others, like the one above, mount using threaded bolts, nuts, and washers. Tighten the nuts by hand until firm; then tighten with a wrench or pliers until just snug enough so that the faucet is firmly in place.

4 Connect the supply tubes to the stop valves and the faucet inlets. If you have copper inlets like these, be sure to use two wrenches, one wrench to hole the inlet still while you tighten the nut with the other wrench. Otherwise, you can easily kink the copper inlet.

One-Hole Faucet

The one-hole faucet is gaining popularity because of its sleek, modern look. It might fit into a sink that is made with one hole. Or in the case of a bowl sink that does not have a faucet hole, it could be installed into a hole bored through the countertop or vanity top. Some of these faucets come with pop-up assemblies like the one shown on page 42, but others do not have an integral pop-up assembly. In that case, be sure to buy a sink body (tailpiece) with

a stopper that you can lift up and press down by hand.

Some of these faucets come with their own supply tubes. Make sure that the tubes will be long enough to reach your stop valves, and that their threaded female ends will fit onto the male threads of the stop valves. If not, consult with a plumbing salesperson to find the transition fittings (and perhaps an extension supply tube) to make the connections.

Some newer faucets have "proximity" valves that turn on when they sense the presence of a hand. Some are powered by battery; others require an electrical hookup.

Installing a One-Hole Faucet

• Screwdriver • Wrench (which may come with the faucet) • One-hole faucet with supply tubes • Drain body with hand-operated stopper

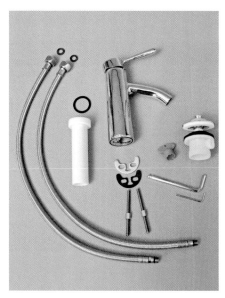

1 Many newer faucets have a lot of parts, so take care to keep track of them all. In this case, the supply tubes are ready to be attached, and the stopper and drain body are included.

2 Insert the rubber washers and screw in the supply tubes (if they are not already attached), and tighten firmly by hand. Also screw in the threaded mounting rods. Screw in by hand; then finish tightening using a screwdriver or the tool provided.

3 If it's not already installed, slip on the rubber O-ring that seals the faucet body to the sink top. Thread the supply tubes down through the faucet hole.

4 Have a helper hold the faucet in position while you work below. Slip on the rubber washer, then the metal washer, and then screw on the two mounting nuts.

5 Tighten the nuts by hand; then use a wrench to firmly attach the faucet. Do not overtighten.

6 Screw on and tighten the supply tubes to the stop valves, and add the drain body. (See pages 56–57.) This drain body has a stopper that fits snugly; you simply slide it up and down to let water out or stop up the sink.

Wall Faucet

A wall faucet extends out from the wall instead of rising up from the sink or vanity top. It lends a touch of European elegance to the bathroom. While a standard vertical faucet can have its plumbing supply lines hidden or partially hidden under the sink, a wall faucet's plumbing needs to be totally hidden inside the wall. Moving pipes inside calls for basic plumbing skills. (See pages 220-25.) It is not difficult, however, and you'll likely spend more time patching and painting the wall.

Wall faucets are a bit unusual, so you may not find one at a home center. They're easy to buy online. (Avoid inexpensive wall faucets made by little-known or no-name companies; they may have valves that are difficult to install.) These pages show installing a two-handle model, but you can also buy a one-handle or widespread faucet.

Installing a Wall Faucet

- Adjustable wrench or slip-joint pliers
- ½-in. Copper or PEX supply tubing

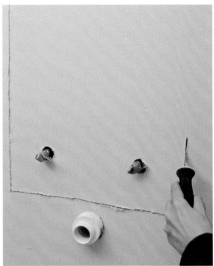

1 Shut off water to the stop valves. (See page 220.) Remove the stop valves; you may be able to simply unscrew a nut, or you may have to cut the tube. Cover the tube stubs with tape. Cut an opening in the wall to get access to the supply plumbing. Extend the opening from stud to stud.

5 Cut tube sections using a tubing cutter, and assemble with fittings as needed. (In this case, one tube travels straight up to the valve, while the other is moved over using two elbow fittings.) Once you are sure of the fit, disassemble the fittings; sand the tubing and fittings; apply flux; and solder the joints. (See page 224.)

• Drywall saw • Couplings, elbows, and other fittings as needed • Wall faucet with valve and trim pieces
• Drill • Tubing cutter • Propane torch with solder and flux • 2-by nailers, drywall, drywall-finishing materials

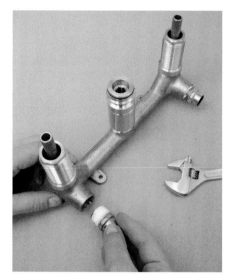

2 Determine how you will attach the supply tubes to the valve. In this case, you'll screw male adapters onto the valve inlets. Use pipe-thread sealing tape to ensure a watertight connection. If you have galvanized-steel pipes in the wall, use dielectric unions to make the transition to copper tubing.

3 Consult the manufacturer's instructions to determine how far back from the finished wall surface you should install the valve. At the desired faucet height, attach 2x4 blocking by driving angled screws (inset). Check the valve for level; then drive screws to attach it to the brace.

4 Cut the supply tubes below the fittings for the stop valves. For copper tubing you will probably need a mini tubing cutter because the space will be tight. Use plumber's sandpaper or a wire-brush tool made for copper tubing to clean the ends of the cut tubes.

6 Attach 2-by nailers to the sides of the studs (inset). Cut a piece of drywall to fit; you may be able to use the piece you cut out in Step 1 as a template. Measure and cut holes for the faucet spout and handles. Attach the drywall using screws; apply drywall mesh tape; and apply three coats of joint compound.

7 Sand the patch smooth. Apply a coat of primer paint, then two coats of paint, allowing the paint to dry between coats. Install the spout and handles, along with their trims.

Stop Valve

To be able to quickly turn off the water in case of breakage or during a repair, make sure you have a functioning stop valve on every supply line. If you have them already and they are in good working order, make a point of "exercising" them a couple times a year to keep them from seizing up. If you don't have a stop valve at a convenient location on every supply line—under the toilet tank, beneath the sink, in the wall behind the tub or shower (usually hidden by an access panel) consider adding one. Or if you have a rusted and very stiff valve, consider replacing it.

The recent advent of push-fit compression fittings has made this replacement much easier. With minimal prep,

these fittings can be easily pushed on to copper, CPVC, and PEX supply lines.

When selecting a stop valve, choose the quarter-turn ball-valve variety. These open and close quickly and are less prone to leak over time.

Shut Off the Water!

Before removing an existing stop valve, be sure to shut off water to it and test to be sure water is off.

Replacing Stop Valves

For galvanized pipe, which is gray in color, buy a threaded valve that fits onto it. Most pipes are $1/2$ inch (inside diameter), but check to be sure; some are $3/4$ inch. To avoid damaging joints, use a pipe wrench to stabilize the pipe that protrudes from the wall ❶. Grasp the valve body with an adjustable wrench, and turn the valve counter-clockwise to remove it. Use a wire brush to clean off any old joint compound or other debris. Apply pipe-joint tape, wrapping clockwise so that as you twist on the new valve the tape is not pushed off ❷. Twist on the new valve, and tighten it firmly using groove-joint pliers.

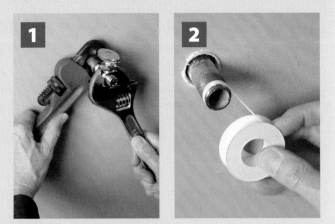

For copper pipe, use a valve with a push-fit compression fitting. To sweat on a valve, see page 224. Copper pipe is relatively soft and can crimp if you crank too hard on it. To safely remove a compression type stop valve, brace the body of the valve with one wrench and loosen the compression nut with another wrench ❶. Remove the valve. Use pliers to remove the nut and brass compression ring. Clean the pipe with an abrasive pad. You may also want to replace the decorative ring. Make an insertion reference mark on the pipe according to the manufacturer's instructions ❷. Push the valve onto the fitting, twisting as you do so. Make sure the valve reaches the reference mark ❸.

Installing Rigid Supply Tubes

• Rigid supply tube • Pipe bender • Measuring tape • Tubing Cutter • Compression fittings • Adjustable wrenches

When appearances count, such as on this pedestal sink, use rigid, chrome –plated supply tubes—sometimes called "risers". The installation is a little trickier than installing flexible tubes, but they provide a much more finished appearance.

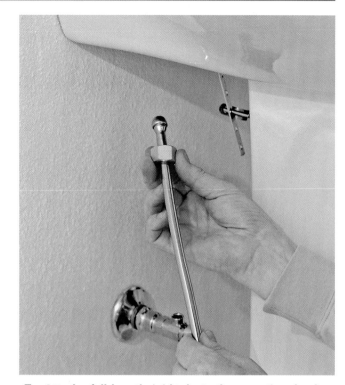

1 Attach a full-length rigid tube to the mounting shank of the faucet using a brass compression nut. Finger-tighten it.

2 Slide a tube bender over the supply tube and gently make a couple of bends until the tube rests against the stop valve. Remove the bender.

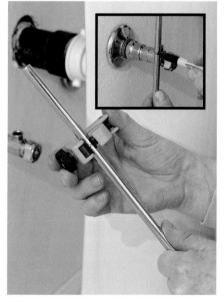

3 Mark for cutting the tube, including enough length for it to fit down into the valve (inset). Use a tubing cutter to trim it to the needed size. Never use a hacksaw—it makes too rough a cut and will crimp the pipe.

4 Slip the compression nut onto the tube, followed by the ferrule. With a little gentle wrestling, work the tube into the valve, and fasten the nut.

Wall-Hung Sink

Simple wall-hung sinks were once common in inexpensive bathrooms. They went out of fashion in favor of vanities and pedestal sinks but are now making a modest comeback. A wall-hung sink lacks the counter space and out-of-sight storage of a traditional vanity, but open shelves underneath provide more storage space than a pedestal sink. A wall-hung sink is often the least-expensive option. And if you need a sink that is wheelchair-accessible, it is the best option.

Newer wall-hungs tend to have either a modern or a retro look. The plumbing will be visible, although it can be at least partially hidden by shelving. If you choose a model with a towel rack in front, it will cover the plumbing most of the time. Still, you may want to install a classic-looking chrome trap and supply lines.

The sink rests on brackets that must be attached to solid blocking hidden in the wall. See page 61 for installing the blocking.

An extra-large sink bowl is great for people who do small gardening projects and don't have a utility sink.

Installing a Wall-Hung Sink

• 2x6 blocking and drywall for patching • Wall-hung sink with bracket and screws • Small level and pencil • Drill-driver
• Faucet, trap, and supply lines • Groove-joint pliers

1 Reinforce the wall with 2x6 blocking. (See page 61.) Refer to the manufacturer's instructions, or hold the brackets in place against the sink to determine where the bottom of the brackets will be. Draw a level line indicating the bottom of the brackets.

2 It's important to get the brackets exactly level so that the sink will be level. Drill pilot holes; then drive screws through the upper slots. Adjust the position of the brackets so they are aligned with the line you drew; then drill holes and drive screws through the bottom holes.

3 Press the sink against the wall, just above the brackets. Slide the sink down so that it slips behind the brackets. Press firmly until the sink is both level and firmly attached. If the sink does not turn out level, remove it and loosen or tighten bracket screws as needed.

4 Hook up the supply tubes and the P-trap. A shelf unit like the one shown here will hide most of the plumbing.

Vanity Cabinet

A vanity cabinet can support a one-piece molded sink, a laminated countertop, or a custom-made tiled countertop. (See pages 68–71.) Most have no shelves or drawers unless the cabinet is much wider than the sink, in order to make room for the plumbing, but see pages 54–59 for vanities with drawers.

A vanity may have only a single cross brace in the back, leaving plenty of room for the wall plumbing. If it has a plywood back, you could carefully drill three holes, one for each supply and one for the drain. However, in order for the fit to be tight enough for flanges to cover the holes, you'd need to remove the stop valves—which would mean shutting off water to the house. Because the vanity back is usually out of sight, it makes sense to simply cut a single large-size hole to accommodate all of the plumbing, as shown on these pages.

Removing an Old Wall-Hung Sink

Turn off the shutoff valves, and disconnect the supply tubes. Also disconnect the trap. Remove the fastening screws ❶. If there is a bead of caulk between the sink and the wall, cut through it using a utility knife. Grasp the sink firmly on both sides, and lift it up and off the mounting brackets ❷. Remove the bracket from the wall. Scrape away any debris and protrusions from the wall. Apply two or more coats of joint compound ❸; sand the surface smooth once it is dry; and apply primer and paint to the wall.

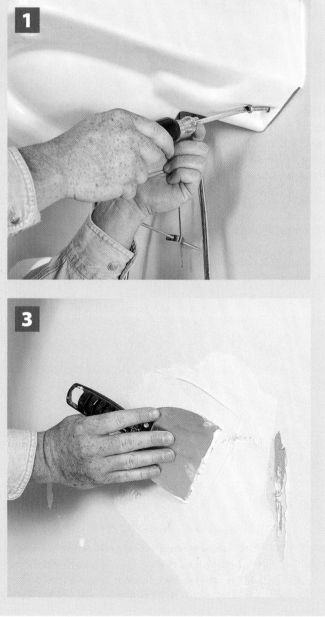

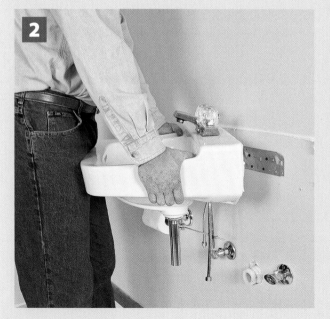

Installing a Vanity Cabinet

• Groove-joint pliers and adjustable wrench • Vanity cabinet • Measuring tape and pencil • Drill-driver • Saber saw • Level • Shims
• Handsaw • Screws • Vanity sink top • Adhesive and tub-and-tile caulk

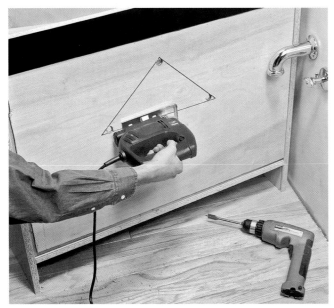

1 Remove the existing sink. (See the sidebar opposite.) Cut the base molding so that the vanity can go up against the wall. Measure for cutting an opening to accommodate the plumbing. A triangular opening is often the easiest shape to make room for the supplies and drain. Drill blade-entry holes at the corners; then cut the hole using a saber saw.

2 Push the cabinet up against the wall, and check for level in both directions. Insert shims as needed, and cut their ends with a knife or a handsaw. Remove the shims; apply glue; and reapply the shims so that they stay in place.

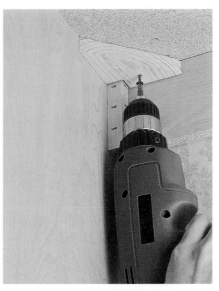

3 Use a stud finder to locate studs in the wall, and drive screws through the cabinet and into studs. Driving screws may lift the cabinet up, so check for stability and add more shims if needed.

4 Set the vanity sink top on the cabinet so it is centered, and attach the plumbing. If the top is made of wood or laminate, drive screws up through the cabinet's corner braces.

5 If the sink top is not made of wood, secure it to the cabinet by applying a bead of adhesive caulk. Seal the joint between the top and the wall with silicone or tub-and-tile caulk.

Vanity Sink with Drawers

Most vanities have a set of doors that open onto a simple large storage space. They do not have drawers below the sink, because drawers would bump into the sink's drain trap. However, you can buy a drawered sink that comes with a special drain trap that neatly snakes a path out of the way of drawers. The sink top has a bowl that is a bit shallower than usual, also to allow for drawer space. When buying the vanity, be sure that the sink and cabinet will match.

Depending on how the plumbing is run, one or more the drawers in a dresser-like vanity, below, may need to be false fronts.

Serpentine drain plumbing allows room for a shortened top drawer and a full-length bottom drawer in this unit, opposite bottom left. Supply lines may need to be moved close to the wall, especially if they come up through the floor.

Installing a Vanity Sink with Drawers

• Vanity cabinet with drawers • Drill and screwdriver • Sink with snaking drain made for the vanity • Faucet with supply tubes
• Groove-joint pliers

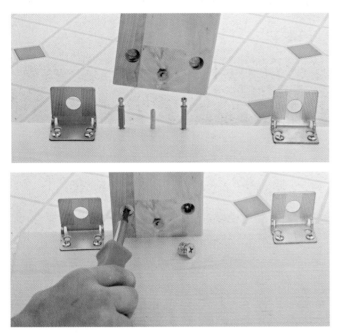

1 The cabinet is typically a "knockdown," meaning it needs to be assembled. Following the instructions, screw in the fastening brackets, wood dowels, and metal dowels. Slip the braces and other pieces onto the dowels (place tk) and screw in fastening nuts (place tk) to secure the connections.

2 Also attach the drawer glides. These are heavy-duty glides that can support large drawers. Drive screws into the holes to secure them.

3 Once the cabinet is assembled, attach it to the wall. This model has legs, so you don't have to cut the baseboard. Check the cabinet for level in both directions. Use a stud finder to locate wall studs, and drive screws into them.

Continued on next page

Installing a Vanity Sink with Drawers, cont'd.

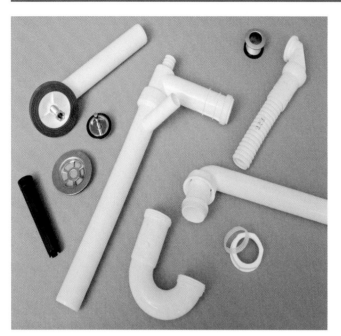

4 Gather the plumbing parts. This system has a hand-operated sink stopper rather than a pop-up assembly, which would get in the way of the drawer.

5 Attach the sink hole flange to the elbow fitting using the tightening tool supplied by the manufacturer. This type has a rubber washer under its flange and so does not need plumber's putty.

8 Set the sink on top of the cabinet, and work below to measure for cutting the tailpiece. Always take steps to ensure that the plumbing is close to the wall, so the drawers will not bump into it. Pick up the sink; cut the tailpiece; and install it.

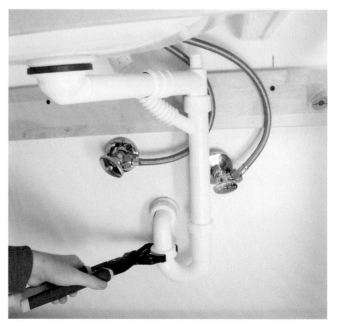

9 Attach the faucet to the sink. (See pages 42–43.) Set the sink back into place, slipping the tailpiece into the trap. Attach the faucet's supply tubes to the stop valves. Tighten all the nuts on the trap. Turn on the water, and test for leaks.

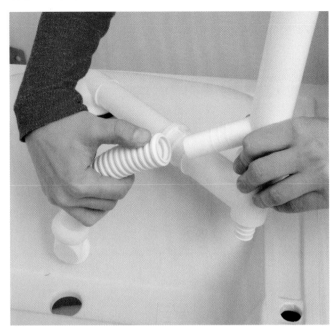

6 Turn the sink upside down, and attach the overflow and the special plumbing parts. Instead of the usual tailpiece that goes straight down from the sink hole, this has an elbow that leads to a tailpiece at the rear of the cabinet. There is also a flexible overflow pipe that simply slides onto the tailpiece, with no washer or nut required.

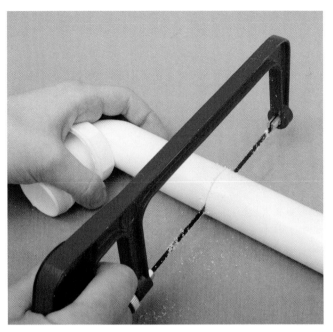

7 In this arrangement the trap arm is very short; it turns downward as soon as it leaves the trap adapter in the wall. Cut it using a hacksaw or backsaw as needed. Use a knife to scrape away any burrs.

10 Install the drawers, and test that they can slide into the cabinet without bumping into the plumbing. The top drawer is shallower than the bottom one to allow some space for the drain.

11 Apply a adhesive bead of caulk to the underside of the sink to secure it to the cabinet. You may also choose to apply a bead of caulk along the joint where the sink meets the wall.

Wall-Hung Vanity

A wall-hung vanity offers contemporary style, helps make the bathroom look larger, and eases cleaning. Plus, most come with drawers, a handier way to store things than the dark under-sink space in a standard vanity.

While 30 inches is the standard height for a vanity, taller people may prefer a vanity as high as 36 inches. The beauty of a wall-hung vanity is that it allows you some latitude. In working out the most desirable height, take into account the additional height of the sink top. Use a level to strike a guideline at the desired height.

A wall-hung vanity and sink top are heavy and must be supported by framing members. Check for stud locations. You may be able to move the vanity somewhat so that its brackets can be fastened directly into studs. Most likely, however, you will have to install 2×6 blocking in the wall. (See page 61.)

Begin by assembling the vanity. Assemble and attach hardware to the drawers and doors, but do not install them in the vanity yet. Complete any plumbing alterations, like new stop valves, while the area is cleared out and easy to work in. Also complete any wall repair, painting, or tiling. Typically, a drain system with a trap comes with the vanity. You may have to add a 1½-inch-to-1¼-inch adapter to the drainpipe protruding from the wall to accommodate the drain system.

A hanging vanity is less imposing than a vanity that reaches the floor. This one has a clever trap arrangement that allows for drawers, like the one shown on pages 54-57.

Installing a Wall-Hung Vanity

• Vanity and hardware • Level • Pry bar • Drill-driver and bits • Screwdriver • Hacksaw • Adjustable wrench • Silicone caulk

1 Determine the distance from the floor to the bottom of the vanity. Make temporary stands from scrap plywood and 1×4s to support the vanity at that height. Set the vanity on top of the stands.

2 Check for level. If the vanity is not level, fasten the topmost bracket at the side that is high. Use a pry bar to raise the low side until the vanity is level. Fasten all the brackets, making sure the fasteners are piercing framing members.

3 Fasten the cabinet into wall studs at one or more additional points along the horizontal rail at the back of the cabinet. Use a stud finder to find the framing members. (See page 61.)

4 With the vanity in place, attach the runners for the drawers. Prep the sink on a pair of sawhorses, and install the faucet and flexible supply tubes. (See page 63.) Also install as much of the drain and trap system as you can.

5 Set the sink top on the vanity, and work out your drain arrangement. You'll have to cut the drain pieces to suit your situation. Remember that on a wall-hung vanity, the trap is located tight against the wall.

6 Follow the manufacturer's instructions for fastening the sink top to the vanity. Some use silicone caulk to hold the top to the vanity; others use brackets. For tops without backsplash or side splash, apply a thin bead of silicone caulk along the walls to keep water from getting behind the top.

Pedestal Sink

A stylish space saver, a pedestal sink is ideal for a small bathroom or powder room. Its cost suits any pocketbook, running as low as $120 for a simple contemporary-styled type, to more than $1,000 for a stunning sink in a retro or antique style. Most homeowners are able to find a quality pedestal sink that suits their style and size requirements for less than $500.

If you've never installed a pedestal sink before, you may be surprised to learn that the pedestal does not support the sink; it is there only for looks. The sink is self-supporting, held by a metal bracket that attaches to the wall. Some less-expensive sinks bolt directly to the wall without a bracket. In both cases the bolts should tie into framing, not merely the wall material. Because studs are seldom exactly where you'll need them, you may need to remove an area of drywall and install 2×6 blocking to which the bracket can be attached.

Installing a pedestal sink is a straightforward job, but if you are replacing a vanity, prepare for some wall and floor rehab. The wall will probably have been painted several times since the vanity was installed, requiring sanding, some feathering with drywall compound, and repainting. Flooring may be irretrievably discolored. You may also want to replace the stop valves and install rigid chrome supply lines. (See pages 48–49.)

A pedestal sink is a stylish alternative to a vanity. It is a space saver ideal for a small bathroom or powder room.

Installing a Pedestal Sink

• Stud finder • Level, pencil • Drywall saw • Circular saw • Scrap of 2 x 6 or 2 x 8 for blocking • Drill-driver and screws • 3-inch general-purpose screws • Scrap of drywall, drywall tape, and joint compound • Drywall taping blades • Sanding block • Pedestal sink • Adjustable wrenches • Faucet with pop-up assembly • Supply tubes • Trap • Groove-joint pliers • Caulk (optional)

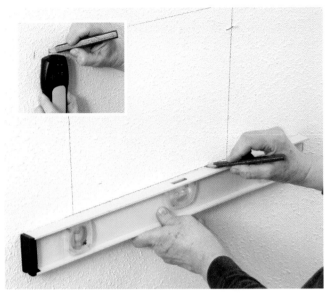

1 Mark the approximate location of the bracket, and then use a stud finder to locate the nearest studs. Using a level, mark for an opening from stud to stud and about 4 in. larger than the brace you will install.

2 Using a drywall saw, cut the hole. Cut a piece of 2×6 so that it fits firmly between the studs. Drill pilot holes, and angle-drive 3-in. deck screws into the backer. Fasten it in place.

Wainscoting

TIP

Wainscoting is an ideal way to cover over the patch before installing the pedestal sink. Be sure to take measurements for locating the backer board after the wainscoting is installed. For instructions on installing bead-board wainscoting, see pages 156-57.

3 Use the cut out or cut a scrap of drywall to fit the opening and fasten it to the blocking with drywall screws. If you will not apply wainscoting, apply joint compound and tape to cover the seams. Let the tape dry before applying additional thin coats of compound—as many as four may be necessary. Sand smooth; prime; and paint.

Continued on next page

Installing a Pedestal Sink, cont'd.

4 Set the sink atop the pedestal, and slide it near the wall. Center the sink over the drain outlet. Mark the top of the sink.

5 Measure the back of the sink to determine the distance from the top of the sink to the top of the bracket. Mark this distance on the wall. Hold the bracket on this mark as you level it. Mark the slotted attachment holes for drilling.

6 Attach the bracket. Drill holes for the lag screws and washers provided with the sink. Fasten the bracket to the wall using a socket wrench (shown), adjustable wrench, or drill-driver with a socket bit.

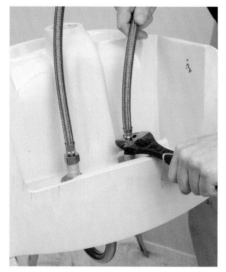

10 Fasten the supply tubes to the faucet body. Twist them on finger tight, and then use an adjustable wrench for final tightening. Pipe-thread tape is not necessary.

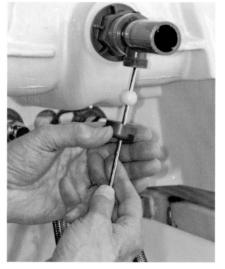

11 Insert the pivot rod into the drain body. Hand-tighten the nut; then tighten a quarter turn with pliers so that the rod is firmly attached but moves up and down without much effort. Insert the drain plug so it engages the rod in the drain body.

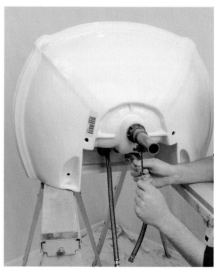

12 Insert the lift rod into the faucet body; slip on the clevis strap; and lightly tighten the setscrew. Push the pivot rod into the clevis strap, and attach the spring clip. Test that the plug closes completely, adjusting the setscrew as needed.

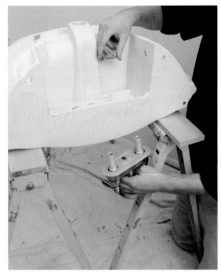

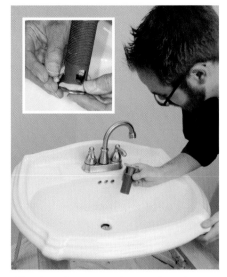

7 Hook the sink onto the bracket, rocking it to be sure it seats. Push the pedestal into place. It should just brush against the underside of the sink as it slides in. If needed, remove the sink; loosen the lags; and adjust the bracket. When the fit is right, tighten the lags and fasten lag screws into the non-slotted holes.

8 With the sink turned upside down on a pair of sawhorses, install the faucet following manufacturer's instructions. Most come with gaskets, but some may require a rope of putty for seating. Attach the mounting nuts.

9 Attach a rope of putty (inset) or the washer provided with the faucet under the drain flange, and push the drain flange into the bowl. Twist the locknut onto the drain body, and then slip on the friction washer and rubber gasket. With the drain body facing the wall, use groove-joint pliers to tighten the locknut. Attach the tailpiece.

13 Set the sink on the support bracket, making sure it seats completely. Attach the supply tubes to the stop valves using an adjustable wrench.

14 Loosen the nut on the portion of the drain protruding from the wall. Slip a nut and rubber washer onto the tailpiece. Loosely assemble and fasten the trap to the tailpiece. Adjust the pipes until they fit together; then tighten the nuts.

15 Slide the pedestal into place. Caulk the bottom for a semi-permanent installation, or leave it uncaulked so that you can slide it out for easy floor cleaning.

Bowl (Vessel) Sink

A bowl sink, also called a vessel sink, rests on top of a vanity cabinet. In the example shown here, the sink itself has mounting holes where the faucet is installed. If you have a bowl sink with no faucet mounting holes, follow the instructions on pages 66–67 to install the faucet onto the

countertop. The other alternative is to install a wall faucet, as shown on pages 46-47.

Remove the existing sink; patch the wall if needed; and check that the cabinet will fit against the wall. You may need to cut the baseboard molding.

Just about any one-hole faucet, including this one with a fanciful handle, can be installed onto a bowl sink. Just be sure that the spout will direct water at least near the center of the bowl's bottom.

Installing a Vessel Sink

• Bowl sink with attaching hardware • Drill-driver • Saber saw • Groove-joint pliers • Screwdriver • Faucet with supply tubes
• Drain trap • Silicone or siliconized caulk

1 Position the sink's template so it is centered on the top of the vanity cabinet, and tape it in place. Trace the outline for the drain and faucet opening, and drill two holes for the mounting bolts.

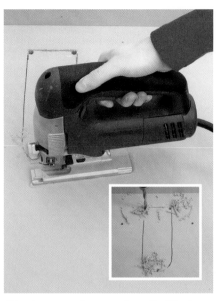

2 Remove the template. Drill holes at the corners of the drain and faucet opening; slip a saber saw's blade in the hole; and cut the opening.

3 Attach the faucet (pages 44-47) and drain trap. Set the sink in place temporarily, and measure for cutting the drain trap pieces. (See page 57.) Turn the sink upside down, and cut and assemble as much of the trap as you can.

4 Apply a bead of caulk to the cut edges of the opening, and use your finger to press the caulk in and cover all of the exposed wood, plywood, or particleboard.

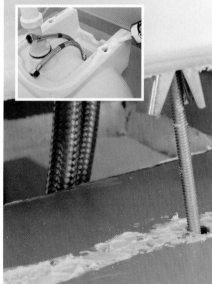

5 Apply a thick bead of caulk to the underside of the sink. Press the sink in place; then lift it up enough so that a helper can slip toggle bolts up through the mounting holes and into the holes in the sink.

6 Press the sink back down, and tighten the toggle bolts. Wipe away squeezed-out caulk. Attach the supply tubes and the drain trap. Turn on the water, and test for leaks.

Bowl Sink with Countertop-Mounted Faucet

A bowl, or vessel, sink adds a touch of elegance for a small price. It takes a bit more effort to keep clean, so may not be a good choice for a bathroom that will be used by children. Here we install a glass sink, but you can also buy bowl sinks made of ceramic (below), glazed cast iron, or copper. As with almost all bowl sinks, there is no pop-up assembly that connects to the faucet, so the drain body should include a way of raising and lowering the stopper.

Some bowl sinks come with all of the mounting hardware you need. If yours does not, consult with a salesperson and buy a mounting ring, gasket, and nut as needed.

The countertop may be made of any material, including wood, granite, quartz, or tile. Use a special carbide hole saw to bore holes in hard materials like stone or tile.

Buy an extra-tall faucet made for use with a bowl sink; a standard faucet will be too short. You may position the faucet anywhere around the sink. The two most common positions are directly behind the sink (below) or at about the two-o'clock position (as shown opposite). If the faucet does not already have supply tubes, attach them. If the stop valves are not close by, you may need to buy longer tubes or tube extensions.

This faucet fits snugly between a gracefully rectangular sink and the wall, increasing the feeling of modern minimalism.

Installing a Bowl Sink with Countertop-Mounted Faucet

• Bowl sink • Tall faucet • Drill • Hole saws of the right type and sizes for your sink and faucet • Plumber's putty • Drain trap to reach the trap adapter in your wall • Supply tubes to reach from the faucet to your stop valves • Groove-joint pliers • Adjustable wrench

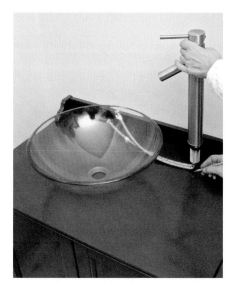

1 Position the sink and the faucet where you want them. (The sink does not need to be centered; moving it to one side can free up useful counter-top space.) Mark for the location of the faucet.

2 Drill the hole for the faucet. If the countertop is wood, you can use a standard hole saw. If you have granite or another hard, dense surface, use a tile-cutting carbide hole saw.

3 Slip the rubber washer onto the underside of the faucet body; thread the tubes through the hole; and have a helper hold the faucet in position as you tighten the mounting nuts from below.

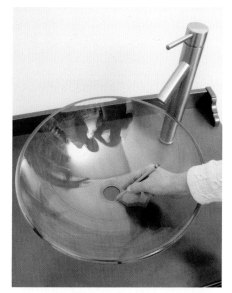

4 With the faucet installed, you can precisely position the sink so that the faucet's spout points to the center of the sink. Mark for the hole; then drill as you did for the faucet, using a hole saw of the right size.

5 Position the mounting ring over the hole, and set the sink on top of it. Slide a rubber washer onto the underside of the drain body's flange (or apply plumber's putty). Thread the drain body down, and have a helper hold the drain in place as you slip on a washer and tighten the mounting nut from below.

6 Attach the faucet's supply tubes to the stop valves, and tighten with a wrench or pliers. (See pages 42-43.) Assemble the drain trap, cutting pieces as needed. (See pages 56-57.) Check that all of the nuts are tight; turn on the stop valves; and test for leaks.

Vanity Sink with Tiled Countertop

Create a custom look for your vanity by covering it with tile of your choosing, then dropping in an inexpensive self-rimming sink. Use tiles made for countertops or floors; avoid fragile wall tiles, which will likely crack in time. The project on pages 69–70 uses natural marble tile, while the project on page 71 uses mosaic tiles.

The edging must have a finished look, so plan this carefully. You can use special V-cap pieces, as shown in the mosaic project, or perimeter bullnose tiles that overhang trim edging pieces. For the marble project, the front edges of the top tiles are sanded and finished. Also plan for a backsplash that has a finished top edge. Depending on the tiles you chose, you may need a wet-cutting tile saw, a saber saw with tile-cutting blade, or a snap cutter.

Bone marble tiles and a pale green self-rimming sink reflect the color of sunlight when it streams through a nearby window.

Installing a Sink in a Stone-Tile Vanity Top

• Plywood and fiber-cement backer board with screws • Drill-driver • Adhesive or silicone caulk • Drop-in sink with faucet
• Measuring tape, pencil • Saber saw • Mesh tape • Tiles, including edging pieces, with spacers • Tools for cutting tiles
• Sander and sandpaper • Thinset mortar • Notched trowel • Painter's tape • Tapping board • Grout • Grout float and large sponge

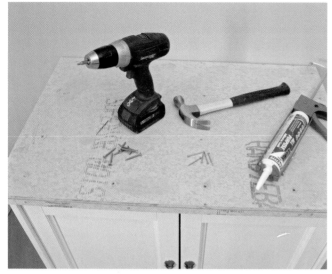

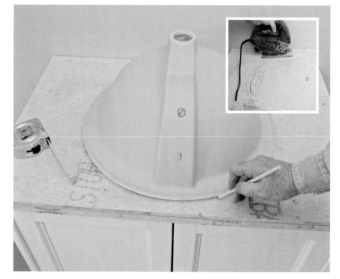

1 Cut and attach a piece of ¾-in. plywood onto the vanity, and screw the vanity into the wall. Cut pieces of ½-in. backer board to cover the top and the edges. Set the backer board in squiggles of adhesive caulk, and drive backer-board screws.

2 Use the template that comes with the sink to mark for the sink opening. Or set the sink upside down, and trace around it; then draw a line ¾ in. inside it, and cross out the outer line. Drill a starter hole, and cut out the sink hole using a saber saw with a rough-cutting blade (inset).

3 Apply mesh tape to the edges. Use a wet-cutting tile saw to cut edging pieces and the top pieces. Measure the top tiles to overhang the backer-board by the thickness of the edging tile, plus ¼ in. (⅛ in. for the thickness of the mortar and ⅛ in. so that they slightly overhang the edging tiles.

4 Set the tiles in a dry run, with spacers for the grout joints. Use an edging tile to check that they overhang correctly on all three sides. Once you are sure of the layout, use a pencil to trace around the sink hole, and mark the undersides of the tiles for cutting.

5 Draw arrows to indicate the tile edges that will be exposed. Use a hand sander or random-orbit sander to smooth these edges. Start with 80-grit paper; then step down to 120-, 150-, and 180-grit. You may choose to go even lower to get a true polished edge, or plan to apply lacquer (Step 11).

Continued on next page

Installing a Sink in a Stone-Tile Vanity Top, cont'd.

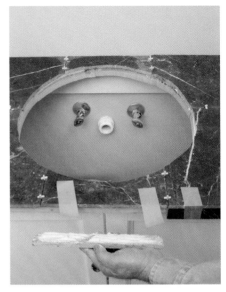

6 To make the curved tile cuts, you could use a wet saw as shown on page 202. Or if the tile is soft enough, use a saber saw equipped with a diamond tile-cutting blade, as shown here. Cut slowly, and hold the tile firmly as you cut to avoid cracking it.

7 Set all the tiles back in place in a test fit with spacers; use an edge tile to check for correct overhang. Remove half of the tiles, taking care not to move the others. Mix a batch of fortified thinset mortar, and apply it to the top of the exposed backer board using a notched trowel. Comb the thinset.

8 Set the tiles into the mortar, again taking care not to move the other tiles. Cut a number of strips of painter's tape to have ready. Apply thinset to the back of the edging pieces; press them against the edge and up against the top tiles; and use the tape to hold them in place until the thinset dries.

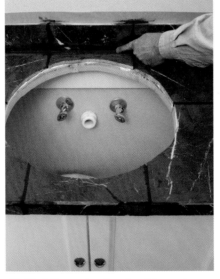

9 Press or tap a straight board across the tiles to ensure that the surface is smooth and even. Remove the other tiles, and install them in the same way. Cut tiles for a backsplash; polish the exposed edges; and set them in thinset against the wall.

10 Allow a day for the thinset to harden. Apply tape to protect the wall. Mix a batch of fortified grout, and apply it using a grout float, first pressing it into the cracks and then scraping away the excess. Use a finger to apply grout to the inside corner.

11 Install a faucet onto the sink. (See pages 42-43.) Apply a bead of silicone or adhesive caulk around the sink hole, and set the sink into the hole. Wipe away any squeezed-out caulk using a damp rag. Use a painter's brush to apply clear lacquer to the edges.

Mosaic-Tile Top

Because mosaic tiles look best when the individual tiles are uncut, it's a good idea to lay out the mosaic sheets and edging tiles in a sample run, and then cut the plywood and backer board to fit, with no visible cut tiles. Here, plywood and backer board are also installed onto the wall, for a thicker backsplash.

Cut and install the plywood and backerboard as shown on page 68. Temporarily tape a few V-cap or other trim pieces on the edges, then lay the mosaic sheets in place with spacers, and mark from below for cutting them **1**. Trowel thinset mortar onto about half of the top and the edges. Install the edge tiles first, starting at the corners **2**. Grout lines on the edge tiles should match those of the mosaic sheets. Start installing the mosaic sheets at the perimeter, and work toward the sink hole. Carefully lower the sheets into the thinset, maintaining a consistent grout line between the mosaics and the trim pieces **3**. Allow the mortar to dry; then mix a batch of fortified grout. Use a grout float to press grout into the joints, then to scrape away most of the excess **4**. Gently wipe the surface with a sponge, continually rinsing the sponge as you work. Allow the grout to dry; then buff the tile surface with a dry cloth.

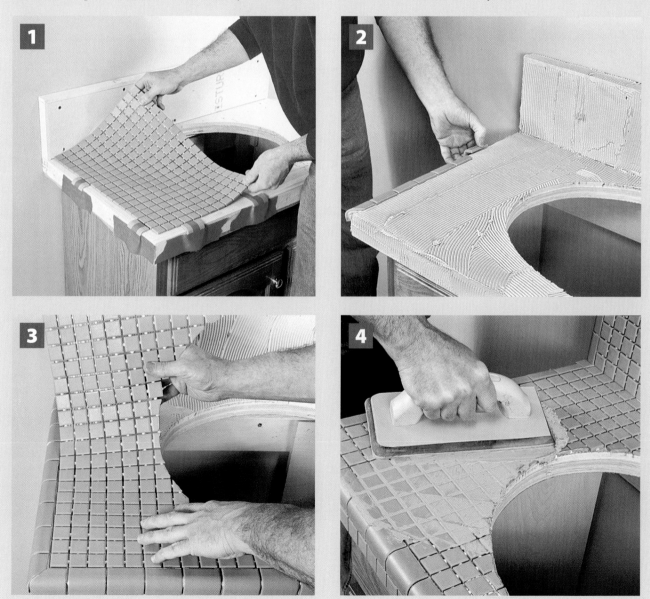

Dual-Flush Toilet Valve

Modern toilets save money by using less water per flush. You can increase the savings by installing a dual-flush valve, which gives you the option of making a one-half-force flush when only liquids need to be removed and a full-force flush at other times. This can save you plenty of money in water costs.

The dual-flush toilet-valve model shown in this sequence, starting at right, requires removing and replacing only the flush valve (the valve in the center of the tank, which sends water into the bowl during a flush). It can be installed without removing the tank. Other types require replacing both the flush valve and the fill valve (where water enters the tank); with them you need to remove the tank in order to make the installation.

Installing a Dual-Flush Toilet Valve

• Groove-joint pliers • Dual-flush valve, which includes the

1 Shut off the stop valve supplying the toilet; flush; and use a large sponge to remove all (or nearly all) the water from the tank. Disconnect the handle's arm from the flapper. Unscrew the nut holding the handle, and remove the handle.

4 Slide on the next part, called the cam adjuster. Slip on the rubber ring, and press it firmly into place.

5 To attach the upper part of the valve to the base, slip it into place and twist counterclockwise until it locks in place.

2 Remove the flapper. In most cases, this is simply a matter of pulling out the flapper's two ears.

3 Clean any debris and grease from the flush valve's base. Disassemble the new valve, and slide the bottom portion (with the rubber gasket) down onto the flush valve. Push it firmly into place.

6 Install the control box on the inside of the tank by slipping the handle's arm into it from the outside of the tank. Keep the half-flush button on top. Hand-tighten the mounting nut, and connect the hose that runs from the control box to the flush valve.

7 Adjust the valve's float. There are two adjustment tabs, one for the full flush and one for the one-half-force flush. Slide either one up to increase the amount of water and down to decrease it.

8 Turn on the stop valve to restore water, and test. If either flush is too weak or too strong, raise or lower the valve's adjustment tab.

Toilet Options

Now is a good time to buy a new toilet. Older toilets used up to 6 gallons per flush, which was wasteful. When regulations went into effect requiring no more than 1.6 gallons per flush, many of the first toilets were notorious for weak flushes. But since then, advances in design have led to toilets that flush well while using a minimal amount of water.

Avoid buying the very cheapest toilet, which likely will not flush well. You need only go up slightly in price—say, $120 or so—to get a gravity-fed toilet with improved design features like a narrowed trapway and large-diameter flush valve. If you want to boost the flushing power more, consider buying a power-assist toilet, which produces an authoritative flush while using as little as 1.2 gallons.

Most residential toilets have basically the same design, with a tank (the upper part) resting on the bowl. However, shape and design differences can go a surprisingly long

way toward defining the look of a bathroom. A toilet may have a Victorian, Deco, or Contemporary look. And some manufacturers make toilets and sinks that harmonize visually.

Removing a toilet and replacing it with a new one is a surprisingly easy job. You can probably find a new toilet with good flushing power and an agreeable appearance for under $200, so there's no reason not to take on the project. (Also, if you install new flooring in a bathroom, it's always best to pick up the toilet, install the flooring, and then reinstall the toilet, rather than trying to butt the new flooring up to the toilet base.)

To quickly and easily improve the look of an existing toilet, replace the handle or the seat. (See pages 80–81.)

Most people take the safe route and choose white for a toilet and pedestal sink, but contemporary colors like these taupe fixtures make a statement and are unlikely to go out of style.

Replacing a Toilet

• Large sponge and a bucket • Adjustable wrenches or groove-joint pliers • Needle-nose pliers • Putty knife • Screwdriver • Toilet
• Wax toilet ring • Hacksaw

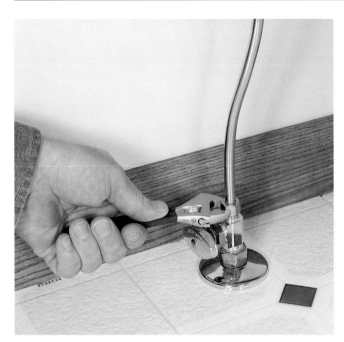

1 Shut off water at the stop valve. Flush the toilet, and use a large sponge to empty the tank and the bowl. Use a wrench or pliers to loosen the nut holding the supply tube, and remove the tube from the valve.

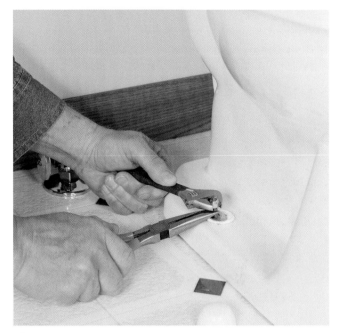

2 Remove the decorative caps that cover the hold-down bolts on each side of the toilet bowl. Use pliers or a wrench to loosen and remove the nut. If the bolt spins, use needle-nose pliers to hold it while you turn the nut.

3 Wiggle the bowl from side to side until the seal formed by the wax ring is broken. Grasp the toilet on both sides next to the seat hinges, and carefully lift the bowl up. If weight is an issue, unscrew the bolts that hold the tank to the bowl and remove the tank.

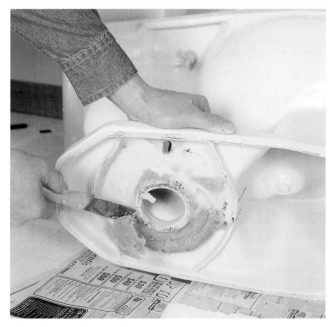

4 If you will reuse the old toilet, place it on several layers of newspaper and tip it on its side. Use a putty knife to scrape away the old wax from the bottom of the bowl; then clean the area with soap and water.

Continued on next page

Replacing a Toilet, cont'd.

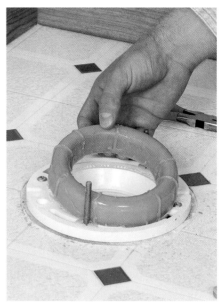

5a If the old toilet flange is usable, scrape away wax from the flange on the floor. Insert new toilet bolts and a wax ring on the flange.

5b If the old flange is broken, install a new one (inset). Install new closet bolts. If the bolts come with washers, use the washers to hold the bolts in place.

5c Place a new wax ring onto the flange so it fits between the bolts. The ring is wide enough so you can press the bolts to its sides, which also helps hold the bolts upright while you work.

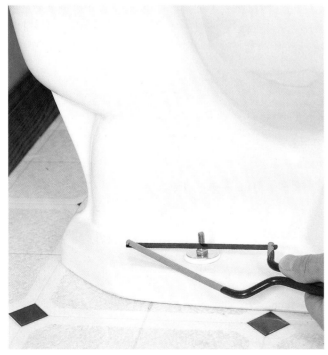

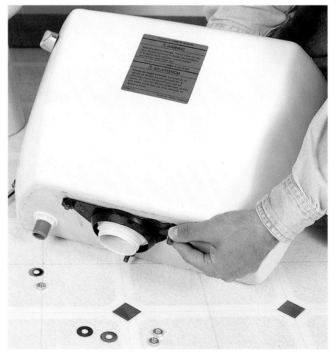

8 If the bolts stick up too high to allow the decorative plastic covers to snap into place, cut them using a small hacksaw. Because this may loosen the bolts, retighten the bolts as needed.

9 Follow manufacturer's instructions for installing the tank. This model has three bolts, but some models use two. Be sure to place the large rubber gasket and the small rubber washers in the right places.

6 Carefully lower the bowl onto the flange, taking care to thread the bolts through the holes. If you make a mistake and the bolt lies down, pick up the bowl and try again. Press the bowl down firmly.

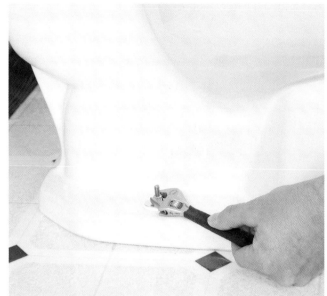

7 Slip the plastic washers onto the bolts, and push down firmly on the bowl. Thread nuts onto the toilet bolts, and tighten them using an adjustable wrench. Stop turning when the nuts feel snug and the bowl does not rock.

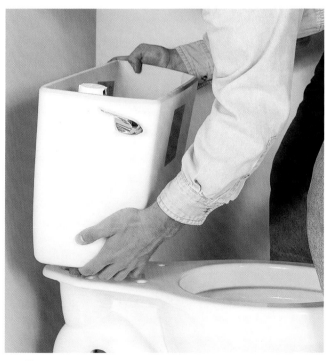

10 Lift the tank onto the bowl, and slide the bolts through the holes. Tighten the bolts until the tank stops rocking; then make an extra one-quarter turn—no more, or you might crack the tank.

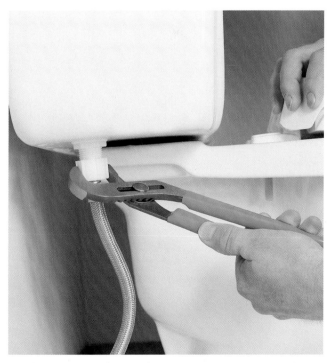

11 Attach a toilet supply tube to the stop valve and to the fill valve at the bottom of the tank. Tighten using groove-joint pliers. Turn on the water, and check for leaks. Flush the bowl, and check for leaks around the base.

Bidet

Long a standard bathroom fixture in Europe, bidets are growing in popularity on this side of the Pond. Many people who use them (both women and men) feel that they offer superior hygiene; for some, they help alleviate problems with inflammation or infection by reducing bacteria. Now bidets are made by all major fixture manufacturers in the same colors and styles as other bathroom fixtures. A bidet looks like a toilet, without the tank or lid. Water is supplied by a sprayer mounted on the back wall or bottom of the bowl.

Installing a new bidet calls for running a new drain line (though usually not a new vent, as long as the bidet is near a toilet), and connecting to both hot- and cold-water supplies. Unless you have plumbing experience, it is best to hire a plumber to install one. Another option is a bidet attachment for a toilet, which can be easily installed, as shown opposite.

For many people who suffer from inflammation or frequent infections, a bidet offers convenient cleansing and relief.

A bidet seat attachment that includes one or two bowl nozzles can be added to an existing toilet.

Adding a Bidet Seat Attachment

A unit like this can be used when desired and will not interfere with normal toilet access. Some bidet attachments are available with cold-water-only plumbing, but the one shown here attaches to both cold- and hot-water lines, so you can adjust the temperature as desired. In most cases, running a line to a hot-water stop valve under a sink is not difficult.

Installing a Bidet Seat Attachment onto a Toilet

• Adjustable wrench or groove-joint pliers • Screwdriver • Bidet unit, which comes with fittings and hoses

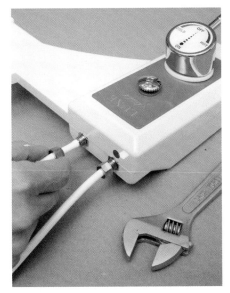

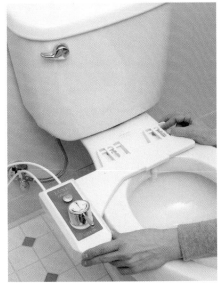

1 Determine the path that the water-supply tubes will take to nearby hot- and cold-water stop valves. Cut the tubes a bit longer than needed, and attach them to the back of the unit. Slip a nut onto a tube; slide the tube onto the fitting; and tighten the nut to secure the connection.

2 Remove the toilet seat. Position the bidet unit, and align the coupling holes over the holes for the seat.

3 Set the seat on top of the bidet; insert the mounting bolts; and screw on the nuts from below. Tighten the bolts using a screwdriver.

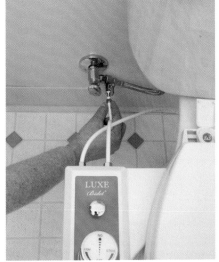

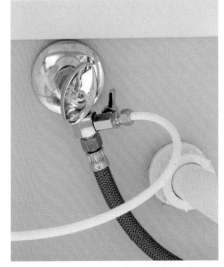

4 Shut off the cold-water stop valve; flush the toilet; and remove water from the tank using a large sponge. Disconnect the toilet's supply tube from the stop valve. (A bit of water will come out of the tube; direct it into a small container.) Screw on the valve supplied by the manufacturer.

5 Connect the toilet's supply tube to the valve, and tighten using a wrench or pliers. Cut the cold-water bidet tube to the desired length. Slip on a nut; slide the tube onto the fitting; and tighten the nut.

6 Run the hot-water tube to a nearby hot-water stop valve (probably under a sink). Install the hot-water valve and tube as you did for the cold-water connection (Steps 4 and 5). Turn on the hot and cold valves to test the fittings.

Toilet Seats and Handles

Sometimes an inexpensive and quick change-out can make a surprising difference. Nobody's saying that by replacing a toilet seat or handle you'll suddenly make your bathroom sparkle, but these small items can affect the general ambiance in subtle but real ways.

It's possible to coordinate your toilet tank lever with other bathroom hardware; chrome used to be the norm, but nowadays darker finishes add a touch of class.

Handles

A toilet handle (also called a trip lever) can be replaced in a few minutes, so there's no reason not to install a new one with an updated style. Brushed chrome, nickel, ceramic, and wood are some possible materials used for handles. Most toilets have front-mounted handles, and—unless you have a very old toilet—these are universal in design, so they are easily interchangeable. If you have a side-mounted handle, buy a new one designed to fit into your model toilet.

Remove the tank lid. Disconnect the chain or clip from the handle's arm, and remember which hole it was attached to ❶. To remove the old handle, unscrew the mounting nut. The nut is reverse-threaded, meaning that you turn it clockwise to remove it, rather than the usual counterclockwise. Pull the handle out through the hole ❷. To install a replacement handle, slip the arm through the hole; then slide the nut onto the threads. Tighten by turning the nut counterclockwise ❸.

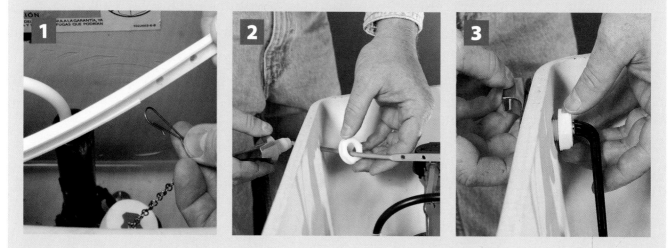

Toilet Seat

Replacing an old, worn seat with a classic painted-wood seat is an upgrade that adds warmth, dignity, and a touch of formality. Seats come in two basic sizes: shorter with a rounded front, and elongated. A few possible features:

- Foam seats have been available for some time; whether or not you find them comfortable is a matter of personal preference.
- Models with slow-close lids and seats eliminate the banging sound of a lid slamming shut.
- Some seats have hinges with an easy-remove feature: just give two fittings a quick counterclockwise flip, and pull the seat off. This makes it easy to clean otherwise hard-to-reach areas.

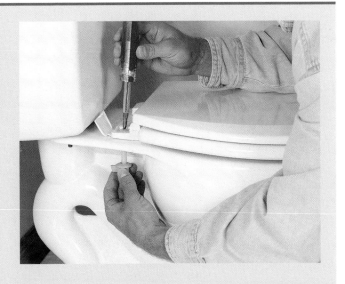

To remove an old seat, flip up the two flaps covering the screw heads at the back of the seat. Use a pair of pliers to hold the nuts below still while you unscrew from above. If a nut is held tight by corrosion (a common problem with old metal fittings), try spraying with penetrating oil. If that doesn't loosen the nut, you may need to cut through the bolt using a small hacksaw or a hacksaw blade by itself; protect adjacent areas with duct tape.

Though unusual, a black toilet seat that coordinates with the room's trim adds a finished formal feel that dresses up the overall design.

3
Storage and Racks

For years, bathroom storage space was limited to a medicine chest and towel racks, with perhaps a drawerless vanity cabinet for cleaning products. Nowadays manufacturers offer all sorts of storage possibilities, including recessed cabinets, vanities with drawers, and shelving units designed to make the most of small spaces. This chapter shows how to choose and install medicine cabinets and towel racks and how to create a recessed niche with shelves. We'll also give instructions for adding grab bars and other features to make a bathroom more accessible.

Choosing Medicine Cabinets

It can be difficult to find a medicine cabinet that makes a substantial design statement and suits your style. In that case, you may be better off choosing a minimalist cabinet—one that has a simple, narrow frame around the mirror.

If you have more-substantial storage needs, consider installing a second cabinet on a wall where there is no sink. In this case, you may choose a cabinet without a mirror.

Plan a medicine cabinet along with the lighting. A strip of lights above the cabinet is common, but lights on each side do a better job of illumination. See pages 170-71 for ideas.

Hardwood shelves make this cabinet, above, just as attractive with the doors open. The shelves can be adjusted to just the right heights you need.

The fluted glass in the cabinet at left allows you to see what's inside but obscures any imperfections. You can also get glass that is frosted, seeded, or otherwise decoratively obscured.

A simple white medicine cabinet, right, is dressed up with crown molding at the top.

Even an inexpensive cabinet, bottom left, can exude style and class if it is painted with a good coat of black lacquer.

A wide cabinet with mirror backing on the inside, bottom right, playfully accents the toiletries and seems to enlarge the room when you open the door.

Recessed Medicine Cabinet

A flush-mounted medicine cabinet installs very easily: find the studs; hold the cabinet in position; and drive screws through the cabinet and into the studs to attach it to the wall. A flush cabinet will protrude from the wall, however, and may have shelves that are not as deep as you need. That's why most medicine cabinets are recessed, or set into the wall.

Wall studs are typically 16 inches on center, meaning that usually there is a 14½-inch-wide space between them. You can buy a cabinet that fits nicely into that space. If you have a wider cabinet or need to put the cabinet in a place that is not between studs, see pages 88–89.

Removing an existing cabinet is usually a simple job. Most are held in place with several screws. Remove the screws, and pull the cabinet out. Choose a new cabinet that will cover the opening. If it doesn't, you may be able to add molding around the cabinet to cover the hole.

Installing a Recessed

• Level and pencil • Stud finder • Drill-

1 Use a level and pencil to mark the wall at the preferred height of the cabinet, usually about 72 in. above the floor.

3 To install a recessed cabinet, mark the opening and drill a blade-access hole in each corner. Drill slowly, and don't push deeply through in case there is plumbing or wiring. Use a hand keyhole or drywall saw (not a power saw) to cut the drywall.

If the trim is modest, a medicine cabinet can look like a hung mirror once the door is closed.

Medicine Cabinet

driver • Keyhole or stab-type drywall saw • 2x4 blocking • Screws • Medicine cabinet • Trim, or joint compound and paint if needed

Watch for Wiring or Plumbing Inside the Wall

Work carefully because plumbing pipes or electrical cables may run inside the wall you are cutting. If you feel any resistance while cutting, cut out an opening in an adjacent place and look or feel for pipes or cables. Cables can often be moved out of the way but pipes cannot. In some cases you may not be able to fully recess the cabinet.

2a To locate wall studs, use an electronic stud finder. Or lightly tap the wall with a hammer or your knuckles, and listen for a change in sound that indicates the presence of a stud

2b Another technique is to drill a series of holes, positioned where they will be covered by the cabinet, to find the exact positions of the studs

4 Remove the drywall cutout. Measure the distance between studs, and cut two 2x4 blocks to fit snugly between them. Attach them using angle-driven screws.

5 Slip the cabinet into the opening; check for level; and drive screws into the studs on the sides. If needed, add trim.

Option: If you will install a flush-mounted cabinet. Have a helper hold the cabinet against the wall, checking for level, as you drive screws that extend at least 1½ in . into the studs.

Wide Medicine Cabinet

A standard 14-inch medicine cabinet, designed to fit between studs, doesn't hold much stuff, so many people install a bigger cabinet or add another cabinet elsewhere in the room. You can flush-mount the cabinet, but then it will protrude into the room. When possible, it's usually worth the extra work to cut a hole and recess the cabinet.

The method shown works for a nonstructural wall. If the wall is "load bearing," meaning that it is an outside wall that supports structural loads or a interior wall that supports ceiling joists, call in a carpenter to install a header to carry the load across the width of the opening. Or you may decide that it's not worth the effort and install a flush-mounted cabinet.

A medicine cabinet that is exactly as wide as the double-bowl lavatory below it adds unity and order to a bathroom. This cabinet includes a handy open shelf.

Installing a Wide Medicine Cabinet

• Measuring tape and level • Stud finder • Drill-driver

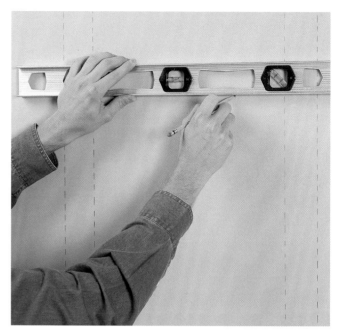

1 Determine the side-to-side location of the cabinet; then measure up from the floor for the height—usually 72 in. Use a level to mark the cabinet height. Use a stud finder to locate the studs. You may choose to move the cabinet over a few inches to make the framing easier.

4 Frame the opening with 2x4s cut to fit between studs at the bottom and top. Nail or screw them directly to the cut studs, and toenail or angle-drive screws to attach them to the side studs.

• Keyhole or drywall saw • Handsaw • Lumber • Screws • Drywall taping knife, tape, joint compound • Paint • Medicine cabinet

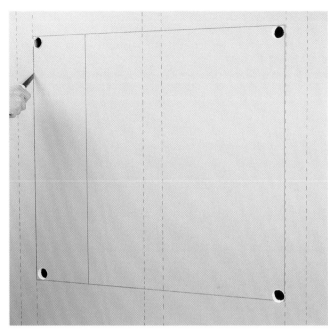

2 Draw the outline of the cabinet on the wall; then add 1½ in. to the top and bottom of the outline for the new framing. Drill an access hole at each corner, and use a keyhole saw or a hand drywall saw (not a power saw) to cut out the drywall. If you encounter what feels like a pipe or electrical cable, stop, cut out a nearby section, and adjust the location of the hole if needed.

3 Remove the drywall cutout, and pull all the nails. In this case, only one stud needs to be cut, but you may have to cut two. Use a handsaw or reciprocating saw to cut the stud(s) flush with the opening.

5 Test that the cabinet will fit into the opening. Nail or screw strips of drywall to cover the exposed studs. Apply joint compound and drywall tape to the seams.

6 Allow the compound to dry; scrape it fairly smooth; and apply two more coats in the same way. Sand the surface smooth; then apply primer and paint.

7 Slide the cabinet into the opening; check it for square and level; and attach it by driving screws into the framing on all four sides.

Towel Racks, Paper Holders, and Hooks

Bathroom racks, holders, and hooks are available in a dizzying array of styles. Most of them are finished in chrome, but brushed nickel, brass, stainless-steel, and other finishes are also available.

You install most of these accessories using similar hardware to avoid having exposed screw heads: attach a small bracket to the wall, and slip the rack or holder onto the bracket. A small setscrew anchors the rack to the bracket.

This all sounds easy, and manufacturer's instructions can be pretty breezy. But it can be surprisingly difficult to install a rack or holder that is really strong and stable. Often the screw anchors (used when you cannot get access to a wall stud) are not very strong. And in many cases the brackets need to be precisely positioned, or the racks can wobble or come apart. We'll show you a few tips to ensure a quality installation that will stay put when people tug at towels.

A strip of hooks, above; a double towel rack, right; and a small towel rack, below, are all easy to install if you work carefully.

Installing a Paper Holder

You install most paper holders in much the same way as you do towel racks. Take steps to ensure that the pilot holes are precisely the right distance apart. Drive anchors, and attach the brackets ❶. Set the holder firmly onto the brackets, and tighten the setscrews ❷. This type of holder swivels on one side to allow for replacing a roll of paper ❸.

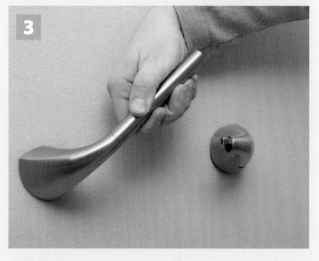

This toilet-paper dispenser, left, has a housing that protects the paper from moisture and provides a handy little shelf.

A two-towel rack, right, holds towels far enough apart so that air can circulate, allowing the towels to dry out well.

Get Everything Level

Especially when two racks are near each other, it's important to get them perfectly level. A discrepency of even ¼ inch can be noticeable.

Installing a Towel Rack

• Stud finder • Level • Drill-driver • Screwdriver • Drywall anchors with screws, or toggle bolts • Small screwdriver or hex wrench for

1 If possible, attach the brackets with screws driven into studs. Use a stud finder to locate the studs, and mark their positions. Many racks are 16 or 32 in. wide, which means that both brackets could be attached to studs. However, you may want (or have) to attach at least one of the brackets to a place where there is no stud.

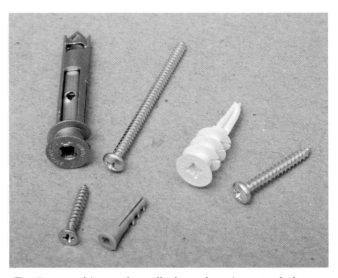

2 For attaching to drywall where there is no stud, the rack will come with drywall anchors. Depending on the manufacturer, you might get a good anchor or a skimpy one that is easily pulled out. It is often best to buy your own anchors. Of the three types shown here, the smallest plastic anchor is not very strong; the white drive-in anchor is an improvement; and the metal anchor, which opens up at the back when you drive the screw, is the strongest. Make sure that the anchor's screw will fit into your bracket's hole.

4 Measure the distance between the marks, and adjust if needed. (The installation literature will tell you how far apart they need to be.) Hold each bracket in place, and carefully mark for the screw holes.

5 Drill holes of the correct size for your anchor, and insert the anchors. Some types get tapped in. Others, like the one shown, are driven in with a drill or screwdriver.

6 Drive screws to fasten the rack's brackets. With some types of anchors you need to keep drilling for longer than you expect so that the back of the anchor can expand and tightly grip the drywall.

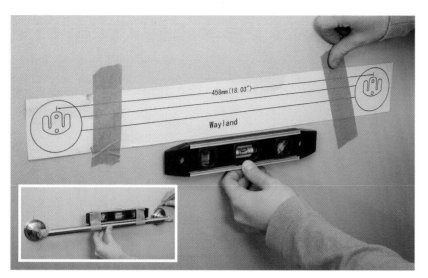

3 If the rack comes with a fastening template (which is a really good idea), tape it to the wall and make sure that it is level. Drill pilot holes of the recommended size for your anchors at the places indicated on the template. **Option:** if you don't have a template, take extraordinary steps to position the bracket holes precisely. Tape the rack pieces together. (They easily come loose until attached to the wall.) Tape a level atop the rack, and carefully mark for the screw positions (inset).

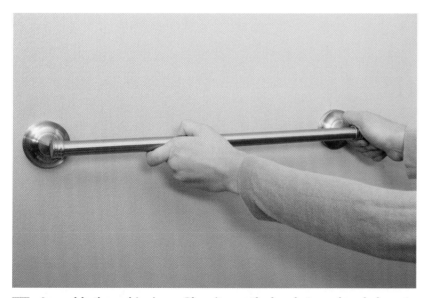

7 Assemble the rack's pieces. Place it over the brackets, and push down to engage it. Make sure both sides are tightly engaged. Use the small hex wrench provided or a jeweler's screwdriver to tighten the setscrew.

Mirror Installation

This wall-hung mirror uses a slightly different mounting system. Drill pilot holes; insert anchors; and drive screws to attach the bracket **❶**. Slip the mirror's base onto the bracket, and screw on decorative bolts to fasten it **❷**.

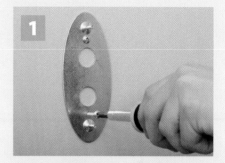

Attaching to Plaster Walls

TIP

An old house may have lath and plaster walls, which means that horizontal pieces of lath, about 3/8 inch thick and 1½ inches wide, run horizontally all through the wall, with ¼-inch spaces between them. If you drive a screw into the lath, it can be a pretty strong connection. However, be sure to drill a pilot hole first, or you may crack the lath. If you happen to drive a screw into the space between lath pieces, try moving up ½ inch or so.

Custom Medicine Cabinet

Basic medicine cabinets are relatively inexpensive, so it's usually not worth your while to custom-build one. However, bathroom wall space is often at a premium, and you can make the best use of it by building a cabinet that perfectly fits the space.

This is not a woodworking book, so we won't show fancy joinery or polished-looking cabinetry; the project can be built using simple carpentry tools and basic skills. The cabinet shown on the following pages may be described as rustic or shabby-chic, and it will complement a variety of styles. The door is the only part that will show most of the time, so you may choose instead to make yours out of a solid piece of ¾-inch birch plywood, then paint it carefully for a more finished look. You can also have a glass shop cut a mirror to fit, and attach it to the front of the door using standard mirror clips.

We made this cabinet using 1×6 lumber, which is 5½ inches wide. You may choose to use 1×4s or 1×8s instead, depending on how deep you want it to be. We used inexpensive #2 pine, which is knotty; you may choose to pay more for clear or "select" lumber instead. Whichever wood you use, carefully choose pieces that are straight.

This rustic wooden cabinet fits with a variety of decors. The pickling stain allows the knots to show through, and a coat of polyurethane makes it easily cleanable.

Building a Custom Medicine Cabinet

• Pine tongue-and-groove paneling, ¾ inch thick • 1×6 (or Phillips and square-drive bits • Angle square • Hammer filler or drywall joint compound • Finish for inside of cabi-

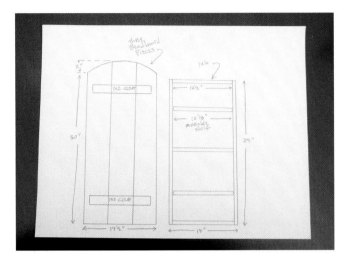

1 Plan the project, and make a drawing showing the dimensions of all of the pieces. The project will be easier if the door is larger than the cabinet by ½ in. or more. Note that the top, bottom, and middle shelves are the width of the cabinet minus 1½ in.; the two adjustable shelves are ¼ in. shorter to make room for the thickness of the clips. (See step 11.)

5 To mark for a curved cut at the top, make a simple compass using a thumbtack, wire or string, and a pencil, and draw the curve.

1×4 or 1×8) for the cabinet body • ¼-inch plywood for back • Miter box, power miter saw, or other power saw • Saber saw • Drill with • Sanding block • Putty knife • Wood glue • Small piece of pegboard • Screws, trimhead screws, and finish nails • Shelf clips • Wood net • Paint for outside of cabinet

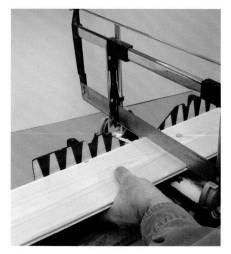

2 Cut and assemble the door first. Make all cuts using a hand miter saw (as shown) or any other type of saw that can make square cuts.

3 Use a circular saw, table saw, or handsaw to cut off the tongue of one of the paneling pieces, to create a more finished edge. You may also choose to cut off the groove of another piece.

4 Push the tongue-and-groove pieces together, with their tops and bottoms aligned. Cut 1×2 cleats 3 in. shorter than the width of the door. Sand the edges. Position the cleats 3 or 4 in. from the bottom and top of the door (so they clear the shelves), and attach them using 1¼-in. screws.

6 Cut the curve using a saber saw. Work carefully to produce a smooth curve. It's OK if you go off the line a bit, but avoid making sudden corrections, which will make the edge jagged.

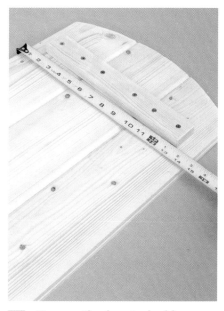

7 Measure the door to double-check the size of the cabinet. Cut cabinet-body pieces so that the cabinet ends up ½ in. or more smaller than the door.

8 Drill pilot holes wherever you will drive screws. Don't skip this step, or you may split the boards.

Continued on next page

Building a Custom Medicine Cabinet, cont'd.

9 Set the four outside pieces on a flat surface, and check that they are square. Attach with three square-drive trimhead screws at each joint.

10 Attach the middle shelf, which is fixed rather than adjustable in order to add rigidity to the unit. Drive three trimhead screws into each joint.

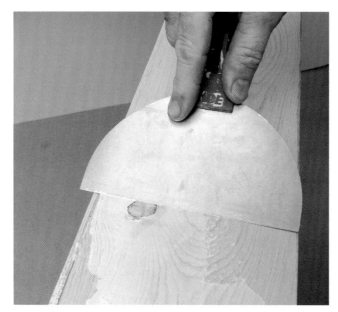

14 Apply wood filler or joint compound to the screw holes and to any open knots or other imperfections that you want to smooth out. Allow it to dry; then sand it smooth.

15 Apply the coating of your choice to the inside of the cabinet and door. Here we apply amber shellac. You may choose to apply the same product as you use for the outside.

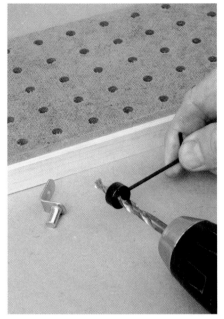

11 Cut a strip of pegboard to use as a guide for drilling the holes for the adjustable shelves. Attach a drill depth guide to a ¼-in. drill bit to ensure that you don't drill all the way through the boards.

12 Drill holes through the pegboard holes. These holes will allow you to adjust the height of the two adjustable shelves.

13 Cut a piece of ¼-in. plywood ¼ inch shorter and narrower than the cabinet. Apply wood glue to the back of the shelf, and drive small nails to attach the back, leaving a ⅛-in. gap all around.

16 Apply paint or finish to the outside of the cabinet and door. We used white paint and water, mixed in equal parts, to create a pickling stain. After the stain dries, apply a coat of acrylic polyurethane.

17 Drill pilot holes, and drive small screws to attach small hinges to the cabinet side and door. Attach them so that the door overhangs the hinges by ¼ in. Also attach a simple magnetic catch to hold the door shut.

18 Once you've attached the door, you can hang the cabinet. It's a good idea to hold a level against the side of the cabinet as you drive screws to attach it to studs in the wall.

Small Shelves and Mirrors

Bathroom accessories like small shelves and soap dishes can cut the clutter in a bathroom and at the same time hit some color and style notes. In most homes, the areas around the sink, tub, shower, and toilet tend to accumulate "stuff" and make the room less inviting. There are a variety of solutions, ranging from open shelves to baskets, opaque boxes, and hooks. If your bathroom is small, storage options that work vertically take up less space—overhead shelves, for instance, or a railing that lets you dangle items with S-hooks. For a small bathroom, a few well-chosen accessories go a long way, and it's best to keep it simple so that the architectural features of the room come through.

An over-the-sink mirror can help set the style tone for a bathroom. Framed oval or rectangular mirrors lend a traditional cachet, while an unframed or beveled mirror has a sleeker, more contemporary feel. A really big mirror will make the room seem larger, always a plus for those looking to sell.

Leaving counter and sink space open gives visitors a soothing sense of open space, and with a little planning your bathroom can have that welcoming feel.

Eggplant-like tumblers, opposite, add splashes of color and share the glinting sunlight with the glass shelf they rest on.

The shelf, soap dish, and dispenser at right are sold as a coordinated ensemble.

Adjustable glass shelves, bottom left, have a bracket system strong enough that they can be used in a tub/shower surround.

When a towel rack is positioned low enough on the wall, below right, a shelf can be placed 6 inches or so above it.

Recessed Niche Shelf

A tiled niche is an excellent way to maximize wall space. It can be a handy and decorative feature on a wall—especially near the sink—or it can be built into a shower surround. While it is possible to build your own niche and cover it with backer board before tiling, prefab niches make the job much easier.

Made of high-density foam coated for thinset adherence, niche shelves come in a variety of configurations (right). To avoid disrupting framing, the niches are 14¼ inches wide so that they can fit between 16-inch on-center wall studs.

After choosing a general location for the niche, find nearby studs using a stud finder. (See page 92.) Bathroom wall cavities can be full of surprises. Before cutting into the wall, drill a ⅛-inch hole, and use a bent wire to probe for any rogue plumbing, wiring, or HVAC obstructions.

If all is clear, use a level to strike a horizontal line where you want the top of the niche. Hold the prefab niche on the line and between the marks for the studs. Trace around the niche with a pencil. Use a drywall saw to cut around the outside of the lines. If you are using ¼-inch backer board, apply it around the opening.

See pages 153-155 for more details on installing the wall tiles shown here.

Pre-fab niches come in a variety of shapes and sizes.

Making a Recessed Niche Shelf

• Stud finder • Level • Wire • Prefab niche • Drywall saw • Silicone caulk • Caulk gun • Painter's tape • Mesh tape • Tiling supplies

1 Carefully cut an opening the correct size for your shelf unit, and test to be sure it will fit. Apply two thick beads of silicone sealant or adhesive caulk to the sides of the studs.

2 Push the niche in place, and hold it with painters' tape until the silicone or caulk dries. Be careful to line up the niche evenly with the wall surface. Don't fasten it with screws—the holes can let moisture in and compromise the tile.

3 Use mesh tape to seal the gaps around the niche. When you trowel mortar to install the tiles, be careful not to lift up the tape. (See page 153.)

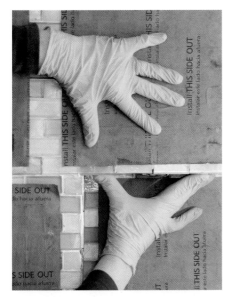  

4 Attach field tiles to the niche's back, then to the sides. As you apply tiles surrounding the niche, overlap the edges for a pleasing appearance. If you are installing individual tiles rather than mosaics, apply bullnose tiles around the perimeter of the niche.

5 Remove any excess mastic, and then apply the grout. Be careful not to let too much accumulate in the corners of the niche. Where a grout float won't fit, use a putty knife or a spatula (inset).

6 Follow the manufacturer's instructions for how long to allow the grout to set before sponging off the excess. Keep the sponge clean by rinsing often. Be careful not to let water puddle in the niche—it weakens the grout. Remove haze using a clean cloth, and seal the grout.

Grab Bars

Even if no one in your household has immediate need of safety aids in the bath, a grab bar is still worth considering: for the sake of guests and family members who suffer an illness or injury, grab bars provide welcome assistance. In a powder room, a discreet support bar near the toilet is a considerate gesture.

Fortunately, grab bars are more stylish than ever. Chances are, you can find a design that will suit your bath decor. In fact, you may want to install them instead of towel bars. (Just remember to reassure anyone who may need to use them of their real purpose.)

The safest way to mount a grab bar is to attach it using lag screws fastened directly to wall studs. If it is not possible to attach both ends, use an anchor suitable for grab bars. The packaging should state that the product is ADA (Americans with Disabilities Act) compliant. Never rely on plastic anchors or toggles

intended for lighter duty such as supporting mirrors or shelves. To equip a bathroom to accommodate someone with serious disabilities, check ADA standards at http://www.adabathroom.com/grab_bar.html.

Grab bars have moved beyond institutional functionality. Style and finish options can fit right into your bath decor.

Attaching a Grab Bar to a Stud

Wherever possible, attach at least one end of a grab bar by driving screws into studs.

Use a stud finder to locate a wall stud. (See page 92.) Find both edges of the stud. Mark the center of the stud. ❶. Drill the hole for the lag screw, following the manufacturer's instructions for the bit size. The bit should always be

slightly smaller than the diameter of the bolt. For example, if you're using a ¼-inch lag screw, drill a ³⁄₁₆-inch hole ❷. Add a washer to the lag screw, and fasten it using a socket driver (shown) or a socket wrench ❸. Attach one screw, but don't completely tighten it. Use a level to check that the bar is level or plumb, and attach the other end in the same way.

Installing a Grab-Bar Anchor

Note: using rubber gloves when working is optional.

Where you cannot attach to a stud, use an approved drywall anchor. If you have plaster walls, check to be sure that the anchor will work.

To install an anchor, begin by using a hole saw to bore a hole according to the manufacturer's instructions. (The one shown is suitable for supporting a person weighing 300 pounds.) Assemble the anchor as needed, and push it into the hole ❶. Hold the guide in place as you slowly pull the tab up and toward you. It will bring the anchor into vertical position behind the wall. Insert the central anchor screw into the mounting plate. Fasten the screw into the anchor until the plate is tight against the wall ❷. Attach the grab bar using the screws provided with the anchor ❸.

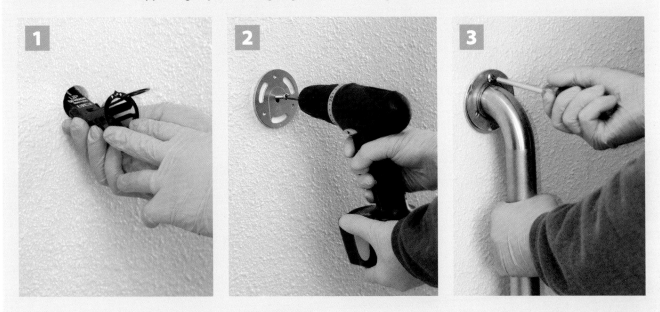

Secure Holding Power

Anchors made for grab bars have enough surface area that a large section of drywall would have to pull out for them to fail. However, forces exerted on an anchor can be unpredictable. If at all possible, attach at least one end of a grab bar directly to a stud. Use only anchors expressly recommended for grab bars.

Where to Put Grab Bars

TIP

Slipping while entering the tub or shower is a common mishap, and most people reflexively grab the towel bar to steady themselves. That's why it's best to position a vertical grab bar or two before installing a towel bar. Small bars of 12, 16, or 18 inches work well, though you may want to install a longer bar to suit both shorter and taller members of the family.

The second priority is providing support in the shower or bath itself. A longer, horizontal bar of 16, 32, or 48 inches works well, but if you need to slant it in order to hit studs at both ends, a diagonal bar will be fine, too.

Finally, a bar next to the toilet adds a helpful assist for getting up and down. Position this bar diagonally with the high end away from the toilet, so the hand can slide naturally while the person lowers his or her body.

In-Vanity Racks

If bathroom organization is a challenge in your home, consider adding some features to your vanity. Pullout shelves and drawer dividers help make the most of every inch of space under the sink. The old saying, "a place for everything and everything in its place" is a good motto for the bathroom, where small items easily go astray. Drawer dividers and small containers help with assigning proper places. Bathroom storage space tends to be tight, and the tricky part is using the most valuable real estate for the most-often-needed items. If the front-and-center space in drawers and in the vanity is occupied by items you use only occasionally—say, shoe polish or big bandages—it may be time to take everything out and put it back together again in a better way. Today's vanities, with nice-looking pullout shelves and drawer compartments, make it a easy to find things, even if they're stored in the very back corner of the vanity. Once everything is organized, your bathroom will feel more useful and will be easier to clean.

Tilted "shelves" in this drawer, above, make it easy to view and store small items like cosmetics.

A modestly priced and easily installed sliding wire drawer, bottom left, allows air to circulate around damp towels.

A pullout shelf system, below, replaces a standard door with shelves and makes everything much more accessible.

This slide-out unit, right, has a hamper that can be easily removed and used as a laundry basket.

Ironing boards can be awkward and space wasting, but a drawer unit, below, makes it a snap to pull out the board and put it away, out of sight.

4
Tub and Shower Upgrades

Posh photos of high-end bathrooms often feature a stand-alone bathtub, with perhaps a separate shower elsewhere in the room. Average homeowners usually do not have separate tubs for occasional bubbly soaks; we have bathtubs that double as showers. In most cases these are 60-inch-long tubs that fit into an alcove, called a tub surround. Though this chapter will touch upon claw-foot tubs, most of its energy will be devoted to fixing up an alcove bathtub. And there's a lot you can do, starting with projects that take a day or less and cost little: refinishing a tub; re-grouting tile; replacing showerheads, handles, and spouts; making a shower curtain; installing a door. Lastly, you may even want to replace a tub or install new shower controls. Most homeowners will hire a pro for this, but we'll show how it's done so you can make sure yours is done right.

Tub Refinishing

Removing and replacing a good-quality cast-iron bathtub will usually cost at least $1,500, probably more—and you're likely going to have to install new tiles as well. It may take a week or so of messy construction to get the job finished. You can save money by installing a steel or acrylic tub instead; they are generally pretty durable, though they can be scratched. Refinishing a tub is much less expensive—$300 is a common price—and it can be done in a day in your home, with little mess. Of course, the results are not as satisfying as a new tub. But if the job is done well, a refinished tub will have a pleasant sheen that lasts 10 years or so, as long as you don't scratch it with abrasive cleaners or sharp objects.

Opinions vary, but most people agree that do-it-yourself tub refinishing kits compromise durability. Because the cost of a professional job is so low to begin with, it's usually best to hire a pro. A search for "tub refinishers" in Craigslist or the Yellow Pages should turn up a good number of companies. Chances are, each of them will tell you that their process is the most durable. Here are some things to look for.

- A good refinisher will supply a number of references. Contact people who had their tubs refinished longer than two or more years ago to see whether the finish lasts or not.
- Most quality refinishers use a two-part epoxy made specifically for bathtubs and sinks, supplied by a company that sells to professional refinishers.
- Ask about the refinishing process. It should include thorough cleaning,

acid etching, and sanding. A special primer should be applied before the final epoxy paint is applied.

- Get a guarantee that surrounding surfaces—walls, racks, sinks, and

the like—will not get sprayed. An experienced professional knows how to protect these surfaces.

- Make sure the refinisher will return if any problems develop.

A tub refinished in black on the outside adds punch to this bathroom.

Follow-Up

Once applied, the epoxy paint will dry to the touch after a few hours, and the tape and paper can be removed. Caulk can be applied at that time, or later. Depending on the type of epoxy, you should not touch the tub for at least a day—preferably longer.

Refinishing a Tub

The photos on these pages show how the job gets done right. You could rent the tools, buy the supplies, and spray the tub yourself. But the total costs are likely to approach that of hiring a pro—and there's a chance that you could make a mistake, especially in spraying, which could result in an unattractive surface.

1 All caulk should be removed. A razor-blade tool takes care of most of this; acid cleaning will remove the rest later. Also, any metal plates are removed.

2 If the tub was previously refinished, the old finish must be removed. Some can be simply scraped off with a razor blade. To remove the rest, heavy-duty paint stripper is applied and then scraped away.

3 Refinishers wear a serious respirator—not just a dust mask—when they apply acid etching compound. An abrasive pad is used to rub the etching compound into all crevices, and then the area is wiped clean with a damp sponge that is continually rinsed.

4 An experienced refinisher knows how far the spray will travel and will cover everything in the line of fire. They will tape protective paper over everything nearby and put tape on horizontal surfaces farther away. A small vent fan will suck out much of the overspray.

5 The refinisher sands the entire surface with 80-grit sandpaper, vacuums thoroughly, then wipes the area with a damp, lint-free rag. Lastly, he will probably wrap his hands with tape (sticky side out) and wipe to pick up the final dust.

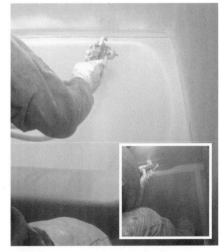

6 Special primer comes in the form of a dampened cloth in a sealed pouch. The refinisher will wipe the primer on all surfaces (inset). Then he will mix two-part epoxy and apply it with a sprayer, allowing it to dry. He'll then apply second and third coats in the same manner.

Re-Grouting

Many tiled surfaces are in sound condition and have attractive tiles but may look ugly because the grout is stained or generally dingy, or it has failed at points. This happens most often around a bathtub or shower. Before you go to the trouble and expense of removing the tiles and installing new ones (pages 132-41), try renewing the grout first. The results may be a pleasant surprise.

If the grout has gaps or is flaking off, you'll need to fix it soon because even tiny holes will allow water to seep behind the grout, which can lead to loose tiles, a damaged wall behind the tiles, damage to wall studs, and even mold. If some tiles have already come loose, remove them, fix the wall as needed, and replace them.

White grout is the most common, but myriad tinted shades and hues are also available. Keep in mind that a grout that strongly contrasts with the tiles will emphasize imperfections, such as misaligned tiles, so it's usually best to use grout that blends with the tile. You can buy custom-colored caulk to match (or at least come close to) the grout colors from a home center or from online sources.

Re-grouting a Tub Surround

• Painter's tape, protective paper, and drop cloth • Scraper or carpet knife • Razor-blade tool • Grout saw • Grout float • Large sponge • Reinforced grout • Silicone or tub-and-tile caulk

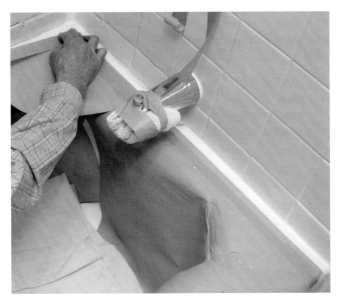

1 Protect the tub by taping construction paper to its sides. Allow enough room between the tape and the wall for using a tool to remove caulk. Place a heavy drop cloth in the bottom of the tub.

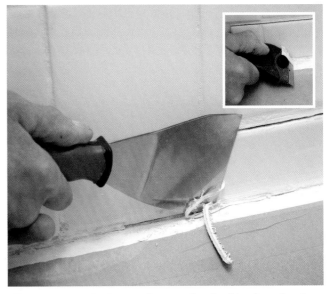

2 If your caulk also needs renewing (and it often does), scrape off most of it using a sharp paint scraper, then a razor-blade tool. To remove the rest, scrub with an abrasive pad dampened with mineral spirits.

Crisp, evenly colored grout lines, opposite, give this tub surround a pleasing sense of order—and they protect the underlying wall as well.

Cleaning Grout

If your grout is in sound condition but stained, try cleaning it. Start with a heavy-duty household cleaner. If that doesn't work, try household bleach or a product made specifically for cleaning grout. If the grout still looks dingy, rent or buy a steam cleaner—which many professional tile setters and cleaning contractors believe is the most effective option. Once the grout is clean, apply sealer periodically to keep it from getting stained again.

Grout Removal Tools

A number of grout-removal attachments for power tools are available. The best option is one that fits onto a rotary power tool (below). These will remove grout quickly, but you must use them carefully. They typically have guides to help keep the cutter between the tiles, but it takes just one slip to damage a tile. For that reason, many pros use only hand tools.

Continued on next page

Re-Grouting a Tub Surround, cont'd.

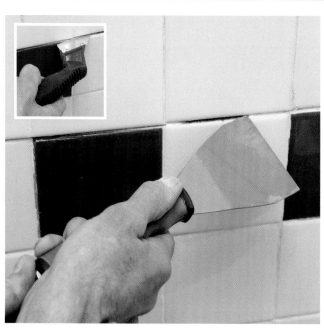

3 To remove the grout, hand tools usually do an effective job. Carefully experiment to find the tool that works best. Often a straight paint scraper or a utility knife is all you need. A grout saw (inset) works faster but could damage a tile if you slip while using it.

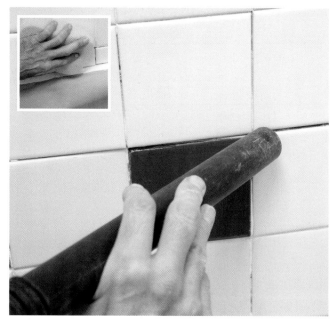

4 Remove grout to a depth of at least ⅛ inch; then vacuum out any dust and particles. Wipe with a damp sponge (inset).

5 Mix a batch of latex or polymer-reinforced grout. For narrow joints, use unsanded grout; if the joints are wider than ⅛ in., use sanded grout. Use a laminated grout float to press the grout into the joints; then tilt the float up to scrape away most of the excess.

6 Wipe the surface using a damp sponge. Turn the sponge over when one side gets full of grout; then rinse it with clear water after a few passes to keep it clean. If you see gaps in the grout, fill them using your finger. Pay special attention to inside corners. Sponge the area several times; allow it to dry; then buff it with a clean cloth.

Showerheads, Spouts, and Controls

Handles, spouts, showerheads, and other metal parts may grow dingy so slowly that you don't notice, so replacing them with shiny new components can make a surprising difference in ambiance. A home center will likely carry a good assortment of replacement parts, and the staff will help you order parts that the store doesn't carry. Shiny chrome is the most common finish, but brushed nickel, brass, and other finishes are also available.

These parts can be installed without turning off the water supply. Showerheads and spouts are universal, but controls and handles must match the size and mounting configuration of the original manufacturer.

Replacing a Showerhead and Arm

You can replace a plain showerhead with a large, fancy one—all types fit onto a shower arm, which is a standard size. While you're replacing the showerhead, consider replacing the shower arm and its flange as well.

Even inexpensive spouts and controls can look great as long as they are coordinated in style and finish.

Installing a Hand-Held Showerhead

A unit like this works well as a stationary head and can be removed to act as a hand-held sprayer. Installation is just as easy as for a regular head.

To replace the arm and flange, screw on the fitting ❶; in most cases, firm hand tightening will make a watertight seal. If not, give it a one-quarter turn or so with pliers. Screw the hose onto the bottom of the fitting (inset). Again, hand tightening will probably do the job. Slip the showerhead into the fitting to use it as a standard shower, or remove it to use it as a hand-held sprayer ❷.

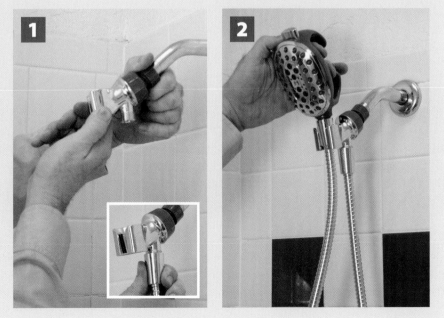

Replacing a Showerhead and Arm

• Cloth • Groove-joint pliers • Adjustable wrench • Screwdriver • Pipe-thread sealing tape • Silicone caulk • Replacement showerhead, spout, and other parts

1 If you will replace the head only, hold the shower arm still, using a cloth to protect it from scratches as you unscrew the old showerhead. If you will replace the arm as well, unscrew it using groove-joint pliers.

2 To replace a shower arm, first wrap pipe-thread sealing tape around the threads that will go into the wall. Wrap with three or four counterclockwise windings (threads pointing at you). Screw the arm into the pipe in the wall as tightly as possible by hand. If you need to screw it further, protect the finish with a cloth as you use groove-joint pliers (inset).

3 To replace a flange, first apply a good dollop of silicone or tub-and-tile caulk to the area around the arm. Slide the flange in place, and wipe away any excess.

4 There's no need to wrap the other end of the shower arm with pipe tape; a rubber gasket inside the showerhead makes the seal. Tighten by hand; then use an adjustable wrench. If the arm threatens to turn too far, hold it still using pliers and a cloth.

Replacing a Spout

Spouts detach and attach in a variety of ways, depending on the pipe coming out of the wall. Remove yours, and take it along when you buy the new spout.

Many "universal" spouts come with adapter parts that allow you to attach the spout to almost any pipe situation. You would use the white adapter pipe shown here, for instance, if you have a short threaded pipe that barely extends past the shower wall.

Before you start unscrewing a spout, look underneath for a setscrew, which is the common attachment method if you have copper plumbing. If you see a setscrew, you'll need to loosen it using a hex (Allen) wrench or screwdriver before removing the spout. Otherwise, use large pliers to unscrew the spout ❶. Use a wire brush to remove any corrosion from the pipe. If it is badly corroded, remove it and buy a replacement of the same size. Wrap the threads with three or four clockwise windings of pipe-thread sealing tape ❷. Screw on the new spout, and hand-tighten it as firmly as you can. It's usually not necessary to wrench-tighten the spout, and it's difficult to use a wrench without scratching the spout. If you find you need to further tighten the spout in order to get it pointing down, remove the spout, tighten the pipe, and reattach the spout ❸. Unless the spout has a rubber gasket at its back, apply silicone or tub-and-tile caulk around the spout. Wet your finger with mineral spirits or water (depending on the type of caulk), and wipe away any excess to produce as narrow a caulk bead as possible ❹.

Replacing Controls

Escutcheons, or cover plates, and handles are usually easy to replace. Buy exact replacements made for your model of tub/ shower faucet. Often mounting screws are hidden under caps that are easily pried off, or there may be a hex setscrew on the underside of a handle.

Tub Overflow and Drain Plates

The round plate below the spout on most tubs covers an overflow hole, where water goes to prevent spilling over if the tub gets too full. This plate and the drain plate are not large items, but your bathtub will look much better if they are new-looking and match the finish of the metal in the spout and controls.

Adjusting a Pop-Up

Most overflow plates have a trip lever that controls either a stopper or a pop-up mechanism.

If you have a stopper (opposite), all of the parts are attached to the overflow plate. If you have a pop-up assembly, there will be linkage attached to both the overflow plate ❶ and the drain ❷. Both linkages should pull out and slip back in with gentle coaxing. You may need to adjust the spring mechanism that attaches to the plate ❸. If they have stopped working, both types of linkage can be replaced with new parts. Or replace them with a toe-lift mechanism. Remove the overflow plate and the drain, and pull out all of the innards. Install the new overflow plate, and screw in the toe-lift stopper ❹. To operate this model, push down and release to either engage or disengage the stopper. Some models require you to lift the stopper up with your toes.

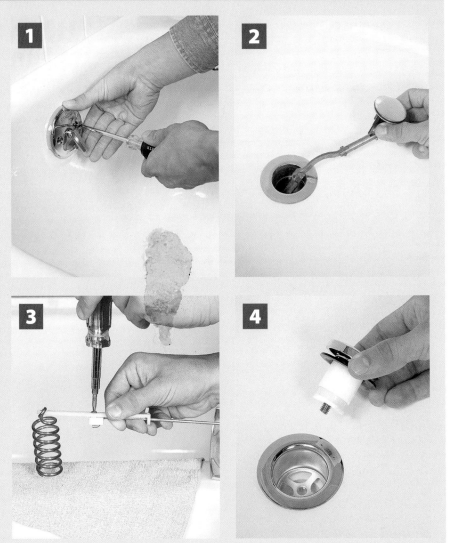

Adjusting a Stopper

• Screwdriver • Needle-nose pliers • Dumbbell • Brush • Groove-joint pliers

1 Unscrew the two overflow cover plate screws (inset), and pull out whatever type of linkage you have. If the stopper was working, you can just clean away any gunk and reuse it.

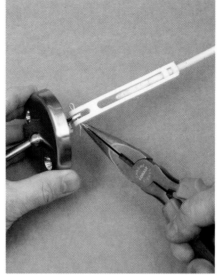

2 If you need a new linkage, finding and replacing it is usually a simple matter. This stopper assembly attaches using a simple cotter pin; open the two parts of the pin to ensure a firm but flexible connection.

3 Slip the linkage back into the hole, and gently thread it down. If it snags, pull it out; give it a little twist; and push it back in again. Reattach the overflow cover plate.

4 You may choose to simply replace the drain stopper. But if you also want to remove the drain body, use a tub drain removal tool, also called a dumbbell. (There are many hold configurations for drain bodies; if one dumbbell doesn't work, try another type.) Unscrew the body by hand, or use pliers if needed.

5 Clean the area around the hole using mineral cleaner and a soft brush.

6 Wrap the threads of the new drain body with pipe-thread sealing tape, and screw it in, taking care not to cross-thread it. (If it gets hard to screw after less than a full turn, back it out and try again.) Tighten the drain body using the dumbbell tool; then add the cover (inset).

Sheet Shower Surrounds

A number of companies make sheets that quickly cover up the walls around a bathtub or a shower unit. Some mimic the look of tile; some have decorative designs; and some are solid-surface sheets with flecks of color. Many of these products include shelves, soap dishes, or racks. They come with detailed installation instructions, which should be followed closely to ensure against leaking. Here are some things to look for:

- Many units come in three basic pieces, one for the back and one for each side. Five-piece units have separate pieces for the corners. Better products interlock tightly at the corners. However, these corners do need to be caulked to keep from leaking. In some cases, molding pieces are included to cover the joints. One-piece units are molded to fit around the tub seamlessly. However, these large and clumsy units usually cannot fit through a bathroom door, so they are used for new construction only, not for remodeling.

- Many plastic (acrylic or fiberglass) units are installed onto exposed framing. You will need to remove all wall surfaces down to the studs, and you may need to install some additional 2x4 framing pieces. Nail or screw the pieces in place; then install drywall onto the walls that are contiguous with the surround.

- Some plastic units can be glued onto backer board or drywall, so you don't need to strip the walls down to the studs. The less expensive types are very thin and give a less-than-substantial feel to your sub surround. But if you caulk them carefully, they can provide excellent moisture protection and an easy-to-clean surface.

- Solid-surface units, which can be glued onto backer board or drywall, are made of a stone-like composite material similar to that used on many countertops. They are typically ¾ to 1 inch thick and so offer a pleasing appearance and solid feel as well as quick installation. These types tend to be the most expensive, but they will probably not cost much more than new backer board plus tiles. And they can be installed onto walls that are imperfect.

This sheet tub-and-shower surround, left, has a raised pattern that nearly matches the tub.

This vinyl sheet tub-and-shower surround, opposite top, matches the grooves of the beadboard wainscoting on the other walls.

Made using thin vinyl sheets that are glued directly onto a finished wall surface, opposite bottom left, this kind of surround typically does not have integral shelves.

This nail-up unit, opposite bottom right, has three interlocking parts that are slid into position and nailed to the exposed framing.

Custom Shower Curtain

A shower curtain is a fun finishing touch that can score big style points. Making your own doesn't require a lot of sewing; in fact, it can be done by hand with a simple hemstitch. If you do have needlework talents—quilting, embroidery, or appliqué, for instance—this is an opportunity to showcase your handiwork. Even a few handmade touches will create a distinctive look. Adding grommets for the curtain rings is easy using the snap-together components shown opposite.

For the fabric panel, the easiest solution is a piece of cloth that is big enough for your needs and already has some finished edges. Scavenged items work well—a sheet, a large tablecloth, or a quilt top, for instance. If you need to finish edges, add an inch to the finished dimensions for each side hem and 2 to 4 inches for the top and bottom hems, depending on how big your grommets are on top. You may want to add iron-on interfacing inside the top hem to reinforce the area where the grommets will be. The burlap fabric shown in the steps was stiff and had a finished edge on top, so no interfacing was used, nor was a hem needed. For best results, hem the bottom of the curtain after you've tested how it looks hanging on the shower curtain rod.

You can slide the grommets directly onto the curtain rod (if it is easy to remove), or you can slip curtain rings onto the grommets. You will probably choose to add a plastic curtain liner, but depending on the material, the curtain may work fine without a liner.

With a custom shower curtain you have an infinite array of color and pattern choices.

A Dry Run

TIP

Before you cut holes in your curtain, test your grommet skills on scrap cloth so you're confident you know how to do it. Once you have cut a hole, you can't undo it, so you'll want to get it right on the finished shower curtain. You can remove the test grommet to reuse it by prying the top and bottom pieces apart with a screwdriver at the little hole in the side.

Making a Custom Shower Curtain

• Fabric for a finished 72-by-72-inch shower curtain, or according to your needs • Thread to match • Measuring tape • Pins for hemming • Pencil or marker that will show up on your fabric • Curved manicure scissors • 12 or so grommets • 2- or 3-inch wide fabric interfacing (optional)

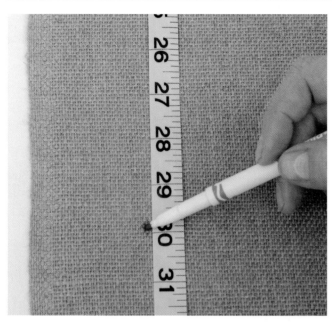

1 Once you have finished the sides and top of the fabric, mark along the top to indicate the center point of each grommet, spacing the marks about 6 in. (or a little less) apart.

2 Use the template that came with your grommet package to mark the outline of a circle for each grommet. Center the template over the dot, and trace in the spaces provided on the template.

3 Starting in the center of the marked circle, use curved scissors to cut a hole through all layers of fabric.

4 Place the bottom (male) grommet section through the hole so that the inside rim is visible. Snap the top piece on.

Shower Door

A shower door offers a more substantial-looking alternative to a shower curtain. It requires more time spent cleaning, however, especially if you have hard water, which will create whitish or reddish mineral deposits. Even soft water may leave water spots and soap-scum deposits. Clear-glass doors are in vogue for high-end bathrooms, but a door made with obscure glass gives you more privacy and helps hide water marks. A typical shower door kit includes channels for the sides, top and bottom, and often requires no cutting for a standard 60-inch bathtub.

Before you start, check that the walls and tub are square, level, and plumb. If the opening is off by more than ¼ inch, doors will make the discrepancy noticeable; you may want to go with a shower curtain instead.

A set of shower doors gives this bathroom a sleek, modern look.

Installing a Shower Door

• Shower door kit, with four channels • Masking tape and saw and miter box (if needed) • Framing square

1 Place the bottom track in the center of the outside tub wall. Tape it in place, and mark each side with a pencil.

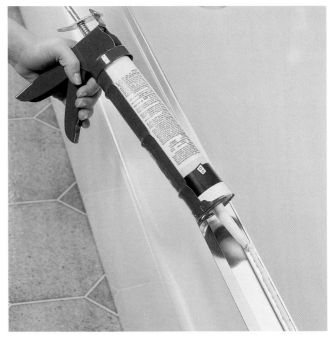

4 Turn over the base channel, and apply a bead of caulk along both of its edges. Carefully turn the track over, and press it down between the pencil lines from Step 1.

pencil • Level • Drill, center punch and hammer • Plastic anchors • Silicone or tub-and-tile caulk and caulk gun • Screwdriver • Hack-

2 Hold a side channel against the wall so that it fits into the bottom channel. Check that it is plumb; hold it in place with masking tape; and use a pencil to mark for the screw holes. Do the same for the other channel.

3 Using a drill equipped with a masonry or tile bit, bore holes for the side tracks. If the bit wanders, use a hammer and center punch to make a small indentation in the center of the hole. Tap plastic anchors into the holes.

5 Apply caulk to the back of a side channel. Press it in place, making sure it locks into the bottom channel in the correct way. Drive screws into the anchors to attach the channel firmly. Repeat for the other wall channel.

6 Attach the top channel to the two side channels using the screws provided. Lift the doors up and then down onto the bottom channel. If the doors do not fit, loosen and retighten the channel screws as needed.

123

Claw-Foot Tubs

A claw-foot tub was a sign of luxury in the late 1800s, and today an antique claw-foot in good condition is a prized collectible. Because the design is so popular, newer reproductions have proliferated and brought the price down. Reproductions may be made of classic porcelain-enameled cast iron (the expensive option), or they may be made of more modern materials like fiberglass or acrylic.

Whether the tub is old or new, many homeowners find that they want to use them for showering as well as soaking. Fortunately, a number of manufacturers offer units that include both showerhead and a shower curtain. These have old-fashioned appeal and offer good protection for your floor and a fairly comfortable showering space.

With some types, the faucet mounts into faucet holes in the tub; with others that have no holes in them, the faucet mounts to the rim of the tub. Or the plumbing may be freestanding, running vertically up right next to the tub. There are also several solutions for adding a curtain-rod unit, attaching to either the wall or the ceiling.

Two standard-size shower curtains are commonly used to get all-around coverage. Check with retail stores or Web sites that sell the tubs for other options, or consider making your own custom-size curtain. (See "Making a Custom Shower Curtain," page 121.)

The faucet will typically mount in a straightforward way into or onto the tub, and the riser and showerhead simply screws into the top of the faucet. The tricky part is mounting the circular (or oval) curtain rod. Most are supported by one bar that runs to the wall behind the showerhead and another bar that mounts to the ceiling. You'll probably need a helper to hold the curtain in place as you attach the flanges that hold the two bars.

If the tub snugs against the rear wall, left, plumbing can be attached to the wall.

This tub, top right, has an Art Deco-like base rather than the more common feet.

Set next to low windows, this tub, bottom right, is a cheery place for an afternoon soak.

An oval window, white wainscoting, and a modified checkerboard tile pattern make an eclectic setting for a bath-only claw-foot tub.

Replacing a Tub

Installing a new bathtub in a new location is a challenging plumbing job, calling for running new drain and vent pipes, and so is beyond this book's scope. Replacing an existing tub is the most challenging job you will find in this book. Most of the work can be accomplished by a motivated do-it-yourselfer; you may want to hire a plumber to make the final hookups.

If the tub is freestanding (like an older claw-foot tub), removing and replacing is fairly straightforward. Shut off the water supplies; disconnect the faucet (which is usually attached to a freestanding tub); and disconnect the drain at both the overflow and the drain hole. Then you can pick up or demolish the old tub. Work with a plumbing salesperson to select the drain parts you will need for installing the new tub.

Most tubs are in alcoves, meaning that they are hemmed in by tiles or other finished surfaces. You'll have to remove at least some of those surfaces, down to the studs, to remove the tub. After reinstalling, you will need to replace the finished surfaces; this will likely take just as long as installing the tub—or longer. Of course, this is less of a problem if you plan to replace the tiles (or other surface) anyway. (See pages 118-19, 132-41.)

Installing the New Tub

Before moving the tub into the bathroom, measure to be sure it will fit. In most cases, the opening will be about 60½ in. wide, allowing a bit of wiggle room for a 60-inch tub. If the opening is too small, perhaps use a chisel or reciprocating saw to cut some studs back ½ inch or so.

There should be access to the plumbing. On an upper floor this is usually through an access hole in an adjoining room or closet. Remove the panel, and use a flashlight to examine the plumbing. On a first floor, access may be

Removing the Old Tub

• Screwdriver • Groove-joint pliers and adjustable wrench • Hammer, chisels, pry bars • Safety goggles

1 Remove the spout, the overflow plate and its linkage, and the drain body, as shown on pages 115-17. If the spout's pipe extends outward, remove it as well. If the control handle or handles are near the tub, shut off the water and remove them and their pipes.

2 Tubs are usually enclosed by tiles or another finished surface. Use a hammer and cold chisel (or a heavy-duty scraper or pry bar) to remove tiles and backer board or drywall to at least 4 in. above the tub in the back and at least 16 in. at the sides.

3 If the bottom edge of the tub is held captive by flooring material, use a chisel or pry bar to remove at least several inches of the tiles. You may need to remove backer board or plywood as well.

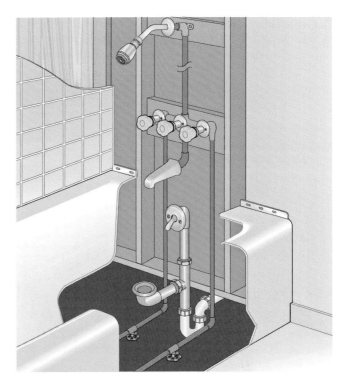

through the basement ceiling, as shown on pages 128-29.

Refer to the tub manufacturer's instructions, which should have exact dimensions for the drain and overflow assembly. Measure to make sure yours will match up with the house's drain trap. In some cases, you may be able to move the trap over an inch or two as needed.

Plan Your Escape Route

TIP

If you remove the old tub in one piece, it can be unwieldy in a small bathroom. You may need to remove a sink, toilet, or the bathroom door to get it out of the room.

Here's a typical plumbing setup for a tub/shower combination. When installing the tub, you need only worry about the drain connection. Measure to make sure your drain and overflow assembly will fit.

4 If the tub is steel, fiberglass, acrylic, or another light material, it may be easiest to remove it in one piece. Depending on your situation, tilt it up sideways, as shown; or tip up one end (usually the end away from the spout is easiest). Place an old blanket or drop cloth under the tub, and slide it away.

5 It may be easiest to break or cut apart the tub. If the tub is (very heavy) cast iron, wear protective eyewear and clothing as you smash it to pieces using a hand sledge. You can cut up acrylic or steel tubs using a reciprocating saw.

Installing a New Tub

• Bathtub • Level, shims • Waste-and-overflow assembly • Plumber's putty • Groove-joint pliers and crescent wrench

1 If access to the back of the tub is limited, attach all or part of the drain and overflow assembly before moving the tub into position.

2 Repair the floor as needed, so the tub covers the flooring. Slide the tub into place, and check for level in both directions. Insert shims as needed. If you are installing an acrylic or steel tub, follow the manufacturer's recommendations for setting the tub in mortar, for greater stability.

3 If you already installed the waste and overflow, skip to step 7. From inside the tub, place a rope of plumber's putty around the underside of the new drain body's flange; press it into the hole; and have a helper hold it while you work from below or from the next room.

6 Join the drain and overflow pipes in the drain T-fitting, and tighten all of the nuts using large groove-joint pliers.

7 Apply a light coat of pipe joint compound to the tail-piece, and thread the tailpiece to the bottom of the T-fitting. This will be a tight fit, so you may need to pull the plastic trap down a bit—just far enough to get the tailpiece into position.

• **Screwdriver** • **Wall finish materials**

4 Place the rubber gasket on the drain shoe, and hold the shoe up against the drain outlet. Have the helper screw the drain outlet into the drain shoe. Finish by tightening with a dumbbell tool or by inserting the handles of pliers into the drain outlet and turning with an adjustable wrench.

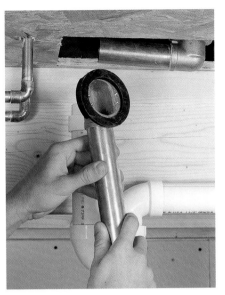

5 Attach the overflow tube (with gasket) to the waste T-fitting. (See next step for the T-fitting.) Raise the overflow tube into position. It should align with the tub overflow hole.

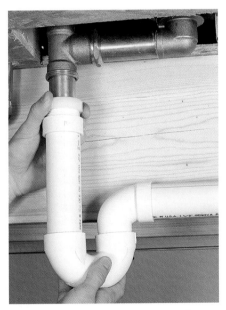

8 Slip the compression nut and washer onto the tailpiece; insert the tailpiece into the trap riser; and tighten the nut to secure the tailpiece to the trap riser.

9 From inside the tub, slip the stopper or pop-up linkage into the overflow tube. (See pages 116-17.) Attach the overflow cover plate to the overflow tube. Install tiles or other wall finish around the tub as needed.

(See pages 116-17.)

Moving a Cast-Iron Tub
TIP

Many people consider cast-iron tubs worth the extra expense and trouble because they have the most durable finish and have a solid feel. However, moving one can be a real bear of a job.

- See whether the company you buy the tub from will move it for you. Even if they charge a fee for this, it will probably be well worth it.
- Plan the drain hookup so you don't have to move the tub twice. Depending on your access, you may need to attach at least part of the waste-and-overflow assembly before positioning the tub.
- Placing the tub on a blanket or drop cloth can work wonders, allowing you to drag it on the floor rather than carrying it.
- Moving the tub up a set of stairs may not be as difficult as you imagine. Just protect the stairs with pieces of carpeting or heavy cloth, and slide it up rather than carrying it.

Making that Drain Connection
TIP

If your drain-and-overflow assembly does not easily slide into the house's trap, here are a few possible fixes:

- If the trap uses slip nuts, loosen them; adjust the position; and retighten.
- If the overflow assembly's down pipe is too long, cut it with a hacksaw. If it is too short, buy a 1½-inch trap extension and cut it to fit.

Tub-and-Shower Faucet

An older tub-and-shower faucet, especially if it is the two- or three-handle variety, makes a tub surround look dated. If you're into the retro look and if the faucet works well, you may choose to simply install new handles, spout, and showerhead. (See pages 112-15.) For a whole new look and more-reliable controls, replace the faucet.

This project always includes some demolition work in order to reach the faucet innards. If you are installing new tub surround tiles, this is a perfect time to replace the faucet as well. If you want to keep and reuse the existing tiles, work carefully. Even so, you may need to replace some tiles.

Start by shutting off the water to the faucet and testing that the water is off. (See page 220.)

Position the shower/tub control where you can easily reach it, whether you're taking a shower or a bath.

Replacing a Tub-and-Shower Faucet

• Groove-joint pliers and perhaps a strap wrench • Grout saw pipe and fittings • Tubing cutter • Solder, flux and sandpaper

1 Remove the spout; if you want to save it for re-use, use a strap wrench. Pry the caps from the handles, and remove the handle screws. Pull the handles off, and remove the escutcheons (cover plates).

4 Cut and assemble all the copper tubing and fittings you will need to install the new faucet body. (See page 224 for instructions on working with copper tubing.) This faucet needed to be brought forward using 45-degree elbows. Install the pipes for the spout (held in the hand in this photo) so that the spout will be at least 6 in. below the faucet body.

• Reciprocating or drywall saw • Putty knife or straight paint scraper • Pipe wrenches • Screwdriver • New tub/shower faucet • Copper • Torch

2 Use a grout saw (inset) to remove as much grout as possible; this makes it easier to pry off tiles without cracking them. Carefully pry tiles away from the wall, shoehorning a putty knife or straight scraper behind them to avoid cracking or marring them.

3 Use a reciprocating saw or a drywall saw to cut an opening. (You may need to add framing pieces for attaching the backer board to which the tiles will later adhere.) Use a pipe wrench or groove-joint pliers to loosen the nuts on the unions. If there are soldered joints instead, cut them using a hacksaw or a small tubing cutter.

5 If possible, install the showerhead above the tiles. Cut a generous opening in the drywall where the showerhead will be, and attach 2×4 blocking between the studs. Run the tube for the showerhead, with a drop-eared elbow soldered to the top of it, up to the opening. Drive screws to attach the elbow to the blocking.

6 Remove any plastic or rubber parts from the faucet body. Sand all of the tubing ends and the insides of fittings, and apply flux to all of the joints. Protect the wall with fireproof fabric, and solder the joints.

Transitioning from Galvanized Pipe

TIP

If you have galvanized pipe in your walls, you may eventually want to hire a plumber to replace them because they will likely rust and develop water-pressure-choking mineral deposits. For now, wrap the threads with pipe-thread sealing tape, and attach dielectric unions to make the transition to copper.

Ceramic-Tile Tub Surround

Changing the tiles in a tub surround is a fairly major undertaking, but it calls for no special skills—just careful planning and attention to detail. If you're lucky, the existing tiles are attached to a solid and straight backer-board subsurface; in that case, you can scrape the tiles off, do a little patching, and start tiling. But most of us aren't that lucky. Chances are, your subsurface will need some repair—or replacement.

Many older tiles are installed on top of greenboard, a type of moisture-resistant drywall. This product is better than regular drywall in moist locations but is not particularly strong and will crumble if kept moist for a prolonged period—which can happen if you have even tiny gaps in grout or caulking. Concrete or fiber-cement backer board makes for a much more durable substrate, and these pages show how to install it.

In a very old building the tiles may be set in a mud bed, meaning that they are embedded in a thick layer of concrete-like mortar. Removing these tiles is extremely difficult: You may need to use a hand sledge and cold chisel—and lots of muscle power. Be sure to wear protective eyewear and clothing as you work.

A large spa-like self-rimming tub may be set into a platform, which can be tiled along with the walls. Temporarily support the tub so you can slip deck tiles under its lip.

Preparing for Tiling a Tub Surround

• Masking materials • Hammer and chisel, putty knife, or straight scraper • Utility knife and razor-blade tool • Chalk line
• Level, shims • Drill with hole saws • Concrete or fiber-cement backer board • Backer-board screws • Wood or composite shims

1 A large amount of sharp debris will land in the tub, so protect the tub well. Tape over the drain hole, and turn the faucet completely off so it doesn't drip. Carefully cover the tub with construction paper and tape, and put a heavy drop cloth in the bottom.

2 Pry away the tiles. Unless your substrate is in good condition, mark walls with lines showing where the new backer board will go, and cut away the existing backer board. Use a hammer and scraper or a drywall saw to cut the lines; then pull the substrate away using a pry bar.

3 Use the scraper, then a razor-blade tool, to scrape away adhesive and caulk from the edge of the tub. Remove most of the material; then clean the tub completely to within ½ in. of the wall framing

4 Remove all nails from the framing. Check all three walls for plumb in several places. If one or more wall is out of plumb by more than ¼ in., the discrepancy may show when you install the tiles. Install shims as needed to make things plumb and square. On an old plaster wall like the one shown, you may need to do extensive shimming (bottom center).

Continued on next page

Preparing for Tiling a Tub Surround, cont'd.

5 At the edges, use a scrap piece of backer board to check that the installed backer board will be flush with the surrounding wall. If not, shim as needed.

6 To cut lightweight fiber-cement backer board (shown), cut the line using a sharp utility knife; then pass over it one or two more times to deepen the cut. Press on the back, and push on the front to snap the cut (inset).

8 To cut holes for the faucet, measure carefully out from the side wall and up from the tub, and mark the intersection. Bore holes using a hole saw.

9 Run a taping blade or scraper over the screw heads to be sure they are embedded; any protruding screw heads can lead to an uneven tile surface.

Option: If you have heavy-duty cement backer board, score one side with a utility knife deeply enough to cut through the embedded fiberglass mesh; then snap it along the cut. On the other side, slice through the mesh to complete the cut (inset). This cut will be rough, so smooth it with 80-grit sandpaper.

7 Attach the backer board using special backer-board screws, which have ridged cutting flanges (inset) so that they embed into the backer board; regular drywall screws will be difficult to drive flush.

10 You don't have to fill screw holes or other small indentations. But along the perimeter, fill any gaps with setting-type joint compound (a dry powder that you mix with water—not ready-mix compound).

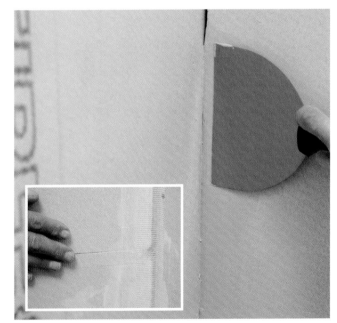

11 If there is a gap greater than ¼ in. at the corners or elsewhere on the backer board, fill it with thinset mortar. Allow the mortar to dry; then apply mesh tape to all joints (inset). Around the perimeter, apply another coat or two of compound, and sand smooth.

Setting a Ceramic-Tile Tub Surround

Installing ceramic tiles around a bathtub calls for careful planning and attention to detail, though no special skills. Thinset mortar dries quickly, so get your ducks in a row before you mix and trowel it onto the wall. Plan the placement of the tiles; making a drawing will help. Practice cutting tiles until you become proficient. Whenever possible, cut at least some of the edge tiles before you trowel the mortar onto the wall. Every once in a while, stand back; examine your work; and make adjustments as needed.

Some people use slower-drying organic mastic for this job instead of thinset mortar. Although mastic works well on other bathroom walls, it is not ideal for use in a tub or shower enclosure because it breaks down when it gets wet. (Some moisture will seep through even tiny gaps in grout and may work its way through to the subsurface.) Thinset mortar is the better choice because it will stay rock hard even if it gets wet.

Here we show installing large ceramic tiles, which can be straight-cut using a snap cutter. For natural stone and other types, you may need a wet-cutting tile saw. Unless your tub is precisely level in all directions (which is rare), starting the installation with tiles resting on the tub will only lead to headaches. Instead, do what the pros do: start with a row of tiles about three-quarters of a tile above the tub, and cut and install the bottom row at the end.

Preparing the Perimeter *TIP*

Apply and sand joint compound where the tiles will end and the wall will start. Plan to paint the wall after the tiles are installed.

Plan carefully for the placement of decorative elements, like these four horizontal rows of black accents. It's well worth your time to use graph paper and plot the position of all of the tiles.

Tiling a Tub Surround

• Level and pencil • Field tiles • Bullnose trim for edges, and corner trims • Plastic spacers, if needed • Plywood strips with one factory edge • Drill and screws • Tile cutters that work with your type of tile • Fortified thinset mortar • Margin trowel • Square-notched trowel • Hammer or rubber mallet • Grout, and caulk to match the grout color • Grout float and large sponge

1 On the back wall, draw a plumb layout line in the exact center of the opening. Set tiles in a dry run from the line to the side wall, using whichever spacers you will use for the installation (inset). If you end up with a narrow sliver at the end, move the center line over one-half of a tile width.

2 Also make a dry run at the side walls. You may choose to have the tiles end either at the edge of the tub or, as shown here, in a vertical row of bullnose tiles the run along the front edge of the tub down to the floor or base molding.

3 Cut strips of plywood or other sheet good, with one (perfectly straight) factory edge, to use as battens. Carefully install them, as level as possible, about three-quarters of a tile above the tub. Drive screws to hold the battens securely, and double check for level. Set tiles on top of the battens at corners to be sure the tiles on adjacent walls are at the same height.

4 After setting tiles in a dry run, measure and cut the edge pieces, so they will be ready to install after troweling on the thinset. Use a snap cutter if possible: Position the tile against the guide (which you can use to cut a series of tiles the same size); press down on and slide the cutter; then push down to snap the tile.

Continued on next page

Tiling a Tub Surround, cont'd.

5 If you need to cut off a narrow sliver, the snap cutter alone won't work. Use the snap cutter to score a line; then use a pair of tile nippers to break the tile along the line. Wear protective eyewear because tile shards may fly.

6 Mix a small amount (here, about one-third of a 2-gal. bucket) of fortified thinset mortar. A margin trowel is a great mixing tool. Once you get a little skilled at setting tiles, you may choose to mix larger batches. If the thinset starts to harden in the bucket while you work, throw out the batch and mix another.

9 Set a few more tiles. Pull a tile away from the wall, and check that the thinset is sticking on at least 75 percent of the tile back surface. If not, use a margin trowel or the flat side of the notched trowel to back-butter a thin layer of mortar before setting each tile. If mortar on the wall starts to skin over, re-trowel it; if it starts to harden, scrape it off and start again.

10 Insert spacers as you go. If four tiles meet in a corner, you can set one spacer in each corner (not applicable in this installation.). Spacers set on vertical lines may come out, but that's OK as long as you recheck the space width. Recheck the lines every few minutes; after that, it will be too late to make adjustments.

7 Mix the thinset to the consistency of toothpaste: it should be wet but firm enough to hold trowel lines on the wall. Use a square-notched trowel to apply thinset to the back wall, taking care not to cover the layout line. Push the thinset against the wall with the trowel held nearly flat; then tip it up to comb long, smooth lines.

8 Press the first tile against the wall by the layout line. Push fairly hard; then give it a twist or slide it so it moves ½ in. or so to ensure adhesion. Position this tile one-half of a spacer thickness away from the layout line. Keep the top of the batten clean so that tiles can rest on them in a straight line.

11 Also check that the tiles form a smooth surface. If a tile is too low or too high, you may be able to fix the problem by tapping it with a rubber mallet or by tapping a straight board with a hammer. If that doesn't work, remove the tile and scrape off or add more thinset as needed. This job gets messy; wash your hands as soon as they get mortar on them.

12 Once you have installed at least half (and perhaps all) of the back wall, move on to the side wall with no plumbing. Start with a vertical row of bullnose tiles; check them to be sure they are plumb as you install them. Install the full-sized field tiles; then hold the last tile in place to mark for cutting. It may take several attempts to cut the tile to just the right width.

13 At some point you may decide to add contrasting tiles, in this case a decorative mosaic band that dead-ends into the bullnose tiles. Install these pieces with the same spacers as you use for the rest of the tiles. With mosaics, check adhesion carefully to be sure all of the little tiles are firmly set in place.

Continued on next page

Tiling a Tub Surround, cont'd.

14 Some bullnose pieces are the same length as one or two field tiles, while others are not. When you near the top of the installation, you may need to cut some bullnoses to avoid ending up with very short pieces. At the corner, install a corner piece with two bullnose (finished) edges.

15 On the plumbing wall, install as many full-size tiles as possible; then measure from them to mark for cutting around the plumbing pipes. If a hole falls between two tiles, hold a piece in place and mark it. (In most cases, the cuts don't have to be precise because flanges will cover them.)

16 Depending on your tile type, use a saber saw equipped with a tile-cutting blade (as shown on page 70) to make notches, a hacksaw with a tile-cutting rod blade, or as shown here, tile nippers. This tool is also called a nibbling tool, because you gradually eat away at the hole, taking small bites.

19 Allow the mortar 8 hours or more to harden. Mix a batch of fortified grout to the consistency of mayonnaise; allow it to slake for 10 minutes; then stir it again. Apply it using a grout float: first press grout into the joints, moving in at least two directions at all points; then slide the float up to scrape away excess. Do not apply grout to inside corners.

20 Wipe the joints using a damp, clean sponge. Work to achieve even and smooth grout lines. Continually rinse the sponge, and wipe the tile surface several times. If a gap appears, fill it with grout using your finger. Allow the grout to dry; then buff the entire tile surface with a dry cloth to achieve a shiny surface.

21 Apply a bead of grout-color-matched caulk to the inside corners. Cut the end of the caulk tube at a slight angle near the tip, so only a small bead emerges. Practice the technique on other surfaces to achieve a smooth joint. Apply the caulk bead; then use a dampened finger to wipe the joint smooth.

17 If a hole falls in the middle of a tile, use a tile-cutting hole saw. Measure in both directions, and mark for the center of the hole (taking the thickness of grout lines into account). Set the hole saw's guide bit on the center mark, and bore the hole. As shown here, a hole saw also works near the edge of a tile, as long as you can insert the guide bit.

18 Once the thinset has begun to harden, remove the batten. Cut a series of bottom-row tiles so that their bottom edges will be about a grout-line's thickness above the tub. Because tubs are usually not level, you may need to change the sizes as you go. Trowel on mortar, and fill the gap between backer board and tub. Set the tiles.

Small Self-Spacing Tiles

Many small wall tiles are self-spacing, so you just butt them to achieve grout lines. It is still important to set them perfectly level and plumb to prevent the problem of grout lines growing progressively uneven as you move up the wall. Fill the narrow joints with unsanded grout.

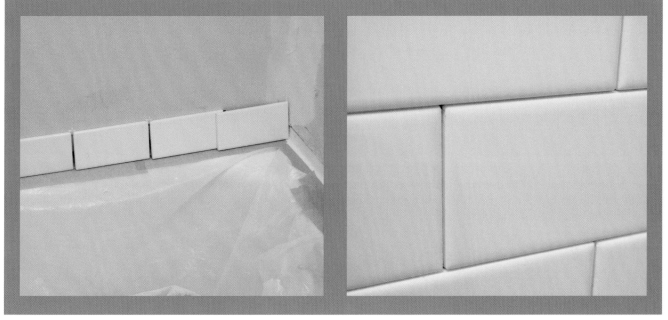

Shower Seat or Shelf

A solid-material corner shower seat is typically installed during the tiling process: Tile up to the bottom of the seat; attach the seat with the anchors provided; then tile around the seat. If you want a seat that is covered by tiles, tile the walls first; then install the seat form; fill it with mortar; and set tiles onto the form.

A shelf made of mosaic tiles adds visual interest, and the pattern of closely spaced grout lines makes the surface slip-resistant.

Making a Shower Seat or Shelf

• Measuring tape, marker, level • Drill and masonry or tile bit • Anchors and screws

1 Apply tape over the areas where you will drive screws to attach the seat form. Measure up from the tub or shower pan, and mark attachment points, making sure that they are level with each other.

2 Drill holes using a masonry bit. The tape helps keep the bit from wandering and protects the tiles from chipping.

5 Smooth the mortar on the surface of the seat. Spread a thin layer on the front edge, and smooth it as well.

6 Allow the mortar to harden and start to cure—about a day. Apply and comb thinset mortar to the top and front of the seat. Here, we are using white thinset.

• Seat form • Medium-set mason's mortar • Thinset mortar • Tools for cutting and setting tiles • Tools for grouting

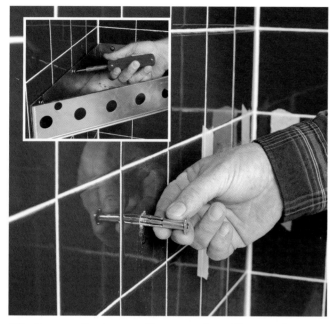

3 Remove the tape, and insert anchors. Here we show a metal hollow-wall anchor; for other types, see page 92. Drive screws to secure the seat (inset).

4 Mix a batch of mason's mortar mix to fill in the seat form. Use a pointed trowel to work the mix into all corners, and poke the mortar in many places to remove air pockets.

7 Cut tiles using a snap cutter or wet saw; you'll need to make lots of 45-deg. cuts, so a wet saw might be preferable. Apply a row of bullnose tiles along the top front edge.

8 Apply a row of tiles to the front of the seat. Here, we use tiles of a contrasting color. If the tiles start to sag, use painter's tape to hold them until the thinset hardens.

9 Allow the mortar to cure according to the manufacturer's recommendation; then apply grout. (See page 140, Steps 19 and 20). Once the grout is dry, apply caulk along the wall (inset).

143

Irregular Stone Tiles

Natural stone tiles with swirls or blotchy patterns and interesting variations make a handsome wall surface. If you seal them once or twice a year, they are water-resistant enough for a tub surround.

Some natural stone tiles are precisely manufactured, so you can install them like the ceramic tiles shown on pages 136-41. Others, like the very inexpensive slate tiles shown on these pages, vary in thickness, have slight irregularities of shape, and may even be somewhat warped. This adds to the rustic charm, but it also makes installation more challenging. You will probably need to use shims (folded-over pieces of cardboard) to lift one side of a tile higher than the other, and you may find yourself often removing a tile and scraping away or adding mortar to its back in order to achieve a smoother surface.

A certain amount of irregularity—the occasional tile that protrudes a bit or grout lines that vary a bit in width—is often deemed part of the look here. But only a certain amount; if the installation is too irregular, it will just look sloppy.

Rough-looking wall tiles, like these tumbled marble tiles, have ragged edges and other imperfections, so installation cannot be precise--though you should work as neatly as possible.

Applying Irregular Stone Tiles

• Slate or other irregular tiles • Power sander • Stone sealer • Wet-cutting tile saw • Thinset mortar • Square-notched trowel
• Tile spacers and strips of cardboard • Fortified, sanded grout • Grout float and large sponge

1 Tiles like these often vary greatly in color. Sort through them, and plan an arrangement that scatters the different colors throughout the wall, rather than having, say, all the gray tiles clustered together. Also pay attention to tile thicknesses; you will need to back-butter thinner tiles more lavishly.

2 There are no bullnose styles for natural stone tiles, so round the edges of perimeter tiles for a more finished look. Sand the edges using a belt sander or random-orbit sander with 80-grit paper. With patience, you can also do this using a hand sander. Then use 120-, then 150-grit paper. Wipe the edge with water to make sure that all sanding marks are removed (inset).

3 Cut the tiles using a wet-cutting tile saw. Apply acrylic sealer to the faces—but not the edges—of the tiles to keep the grout from staining the tile (right).

4 Follow most of the instructions on pages 136-41 to lay out the job and install tiles on a batten. If tiles vary in thickness, start with a thick tile; you can always add more mortar to the back of thinner tiles. Apply thinset mortar to both the wall and the backs of the tiles.

5 Cut plenty of cardboard strips, about 1 by 2 inches, to use as spacers. Use folded-over strips in most places; in other places you may need to double up. Allow a day for the thinset to harden; then apply grout. (See page 140, Steps 19 and 20.)

145

5
Walls, Ceilings, and Windows

Most bathrooms are small spaces, which means that walls, windows, and maybe even ceilings will come in for close scrutiny. It also means that you may be able to afford high-end wall tiles and other treatments because you'll need only a small amount of them. This chapter shows how to straighten out and beautify walls with paint, as well as how to install the two most popular bathroom wall coverings: tile and bead-board wainscoting. You'll also find ways to spruce up a window, as well as instructions for bringing in natural light using a solar light tube.

Wall Prep

The quickest and most economical way to make old walls feel like new is to apply a fresh coat of paint. Before you paint, however, take the time to smooth out any imperfections in your walls. Remember that the higher the paint's gloss, the more it will show imperfections.

If you have only a few minor holes that need filling, use vinyl spackling compound, which is vinyl-reinforced for flexibility and dries quickly. If you have quite a few cosmetic problems, use ready-mix drywall joint compound. For filling larger holes and ensuring against cracks, use setting-type joint compound, which comes in a dry powder that you mix with water; it is the strongest.

Patching Small Problems

If you have visible screws or nails, tap them in with a hammer. Scrape or chip away any other protrusions; then work to fill in depressions.

Preparing a Wall

> • Hammer • Taping knives • Vinyl spackling or joint compound

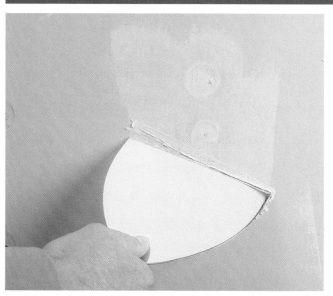

1 **Scoop some spackling or joint compound onto a 6-in. taping knife, and hold the blade nearly flat as you scrape it over the depression. Then tilt the blade up, and scrape so as to smooth it. Feather out the edges to reduce the amount of sanding you will need to do.**

Solving Larger Problems

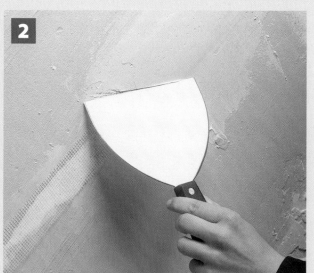

Use a knife to clean out any cracks or large holes. Use a damp cloth to remove all dust. Fill any deep depressions with setting-type joint compound, and allow it to dry. Apply fiberglass mesh tape ❶. Flatten the tape with your fingers and then with a taping knife. Apply a layer of setting-type joint compound over the tape, feathering the edges ❷. Allow it to dry, and sand it smooth. Apply two or more coats of joint compound, and sand it smooth after it dries.

• Sanding block and sandpaper • Fiberglass mesh drywall tape • Primer

2 Allow the compound to dry; then sand it smooth using a sanding block and 100-grit sandpaper. Feel the surface with your hand, and examine it with a strong light to uncover any indentations and imperfections. If needed, apply another coat and repeat.

3 Apply primer to all of the patched areas. Latex primer works fine for most areas, but if there are stains, use alcohol-based primer (white shellac).

Preparing Woodwork for Painting

If your woodwork is alligator-skinned from many coats of paint or if it is generally rough, it may be best to replace it. But minor problems can be solved using wood filler or caulk.

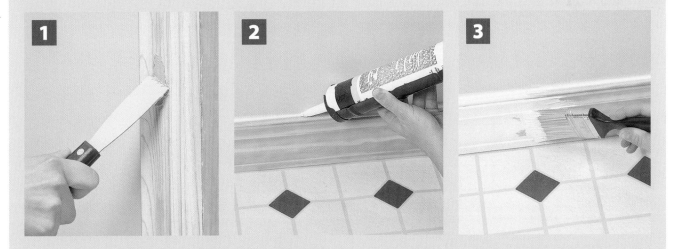

Use a nail set to set any protruding nailheads. Use a putty knife to apply wood filler or vinyl spackling compound ❶; allow it to dry; and sand it smooth. Use latex caulk to fill joints between trim boards and walls ❷. Apply a thin bead; then run a wet finger over the bead to make it perfectly smooth. For either new wood or wood that has been patched, apply a latex or alkyd primer ❸. Allow it to dry; then look closely for imperfections. Sand and fill again if needed.

Painting

In most cases, two good coats of paint should be applied to achieve full coverage. (The wall may look "fine" after one coat, but often there will be small gaps in the coverage that subtly telegraph "amateur.") Use good-quality paintbrushes and rollers for ease of application and a consistent finish. A roller with a ½-inch nap will produce a pronounced stipple (slightly bumpy surface) that helps hide imperfections; use a roller with a ¼- or ⅜-inch nap for a very smooth or only slightly stippled surface. It's almost always best to "cut in" the edges using a brush and then paint the walls using a roller for a more consistent-looking surface.

Neatly painted walls, with crisp lines at the woodwork, no drip marks, and a consistent stipple, convey a sense of professionalism. Imperfections telegraph a subtle but real sense of sloppiness.

Painting Walls

• Drop cloths and work lamp • Screwdriver • Paint & paintbrush

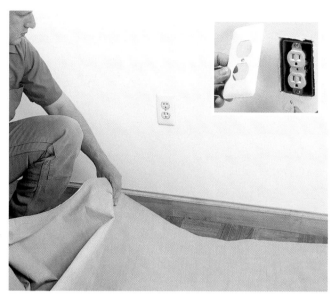

1 No matter how carefully you work, there will be spatters. Remove any furniture from the room. Cover the floor with drop cloths or construction paper and tape. Cover the toilet, sink, and tub as well. Remove all electrical cover plates (inset), as well as any light fixtures.

5 Begin by rolling near the top of the wall, and move down. Using an extension pole, you can roll the entire wall without using a ladder. Roll fairly slowly to reduce spattering.

• Paint roller, pan, and extension pole

2 Use work lights or extra lamps to make the room brighter than it will be in normal use, so you can easily spot any problems. Remove shades from any lamps to get the brightest light on the walls.

3 Use a trim brush to cut in where walls meet the ceiling, at corners, and around trimwork. Dip the brush; then wipe off excess paint. Use smooth strokes, starting away from the woodwork and then applying a line next to the woodwork. Then brush outward at right angles to produce a strip about 3 in. wide (inset).

4 Once all of the cutting-in is done, fill the well (but not the ribbed portion) of a paint pan. Put a roller sleeve and an extension pole onto a paint roller. Run the roller lightly over the paint and then over the ribs, and repeat until the roller sleeve is evenly coated.

6 Reload, and apply a second strip about 12 in. away from the first, starting at the bottom of the wall and moving up. (This applies about the same amount of paint at the top, middle, and bottom). Then spread the paint from the strips into the area between. Reload if needed.

7 Finish by using an empty roller in long, smooth strokes from top to bottom. Shine a bright light to check that the roller laps aren't visible. If you see bare spots, partially load the roller and cover the spot; reduce pressure, and lift off as needed to feather the strokes to eliminate lap lines.

151

Glass Tiles

Glass tile has a luminous look that adds an extra dimension to a bathroom. It is a classy material that adds subtle color, texture, and contemporary styling. You can find some good-looking glass tile for $5 per square foot or less, but designer options can run up to $30 per square foot. If you really like the high-end stuff, consider tiling only the "wet" wall of your bathroom behind the vanity and toilet.

Glass tile is more challenging to install than ceramic tile. Because it is translucent, you must use white thinset; gray thinset will muddy the appearance, and organic mastic will yellow in time. Because of its smooth surface, glass adheres to the thinset less readily, requiring a stiff mix and long curing time. In addition, thinset can't simply be applied with a grooved trowel; it must be smoothed so that the ridges don't show through the glass.

Glass tiles can be applied to cement board or drywall. (Due to its expansion and contraction, plywood isn't a viable substrate.) Plan your layout in advance to ensure that you don't end up with small slivers of tile on either side or at the top or bottom of the wall. Prepare by marking horizontal and vertical centerlines. Then mark lines every foot horizontally and vertically to guide your installation.

Muted color and subtle beauty are the hallmarks of mosaic glass tile. Although more difficult to install than ceramic tile, glass tile's contemporary good looks are worth the effort.

Applying Glass Tiles

• Thinset suitable for glass tile • Notched/flat trowel • Glass tiles (usually, in mosaic sheets) • Wheeled nippers or wet tile cutter • Beater block made of 2-by wrapped with old towel • Rubber mallet • Grout • Grout float • Grout knife • Cheesecloth • Sponge

1 Using the flat side of a trowel, apply a base coat of thinset to a 3-by-3-ft. quadrant in the center of the wall. Next, using a ¼-in. notched trowel, comb the thinset horizontally, keeping the groove depth as consistent as possible.

2 To eliminate any grooves that might show through the glass tile, use the flat side of the trowel to flatten the grooves. Aim for a smooth layer approximately ⅛-in. thick.

3 With the paper side toward you, apply the mosaic sheets. Use light, even pressure to eliminate any voids. Apply each subsequent sheet so that grout joints line up and are a consistent width. As you complete a 3-by-3-ft. area, apply thinset to the next area and apply more sheets.

4 To set the tiles and even out the surface, use a wooden beater block wrapped with an old towel. Tap the block lightly using a rubber mallet.

Continued on next page

Applying Glass Tiles, cont'd.

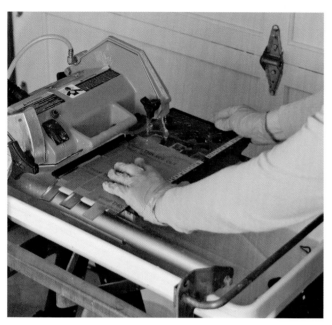

5 Where necessary, mark tile sheets and cut them using a wet tile saw. As you apply sheets, stand back and look for any telltale gaps where the sheets join, and make any needed adjustments.

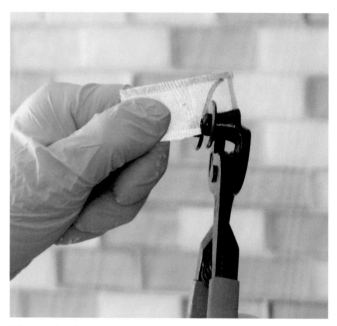

6 A wheeled nipper (shown) or a nibbler may be necessary to trim tiles that surround an electrical box or protruding pipe.

9 Follow the thinset manufacturer's recommended curing time prior to cleaning and grouting. Using a lightly abrasive sponge or nylon brush, scrub any remaining paper and glue from the surface of the tile. Allow the wall to dry completely prior to grouting.

10 Use sanded grout mixed according to the manufacturer's instructions. Apply the grout using a rubber float, forcing grout completely into the joints. Because glass tile is impervious, the grout will take longer to set than with ceramic tiles.

7 After installing the tile, allow 12 hours of drying time to be sure that all of the tiles adhere; then spray the paper backing repeatedly. Once the paper has absorbed the water, start at a corner and peel off the sheet.

8 Scrape away excess thinset using a grout knife, single-edged razor blade, or wood chisel. Don't panic if some tiles pop off. Glue them back into place using thinset.

11 After about 20 minutes' drying time, use a clean, dry cheesecloth to wick moisture from the grout without washing out the grout joints. Allow the grout joints to set up a second time. When the grout turns dull, smooth it using a slightly damp sponge. Use a clean, soft cloth to remove any haze.

Long rectangular tiles are usually run horizontally, but consider running them vertically for an uplifting feeling.

Bead-Board Wainscoting

The word "wainscoting" refers to paneling that covers the bottom third or so of a wall. Bead-board wainscoting has a tidy Victorian appeal that is at the same time casual and inviting. Once painted or sealed, bead board is an easy-to-clean surface that is more durable than a painted wall.

There are several bead-board options. For the full-on cabin look, use ¾-inch-thick pine bead board (used to make the door for the medicine cabinet shown on pages 94-97). This product is usually stained lightly and sealed, though you can paint it. You'll need a simple baseboard at the bottom and chair rail at the top. Home centers often sell ⅜-inch-thick pine bead board, as well as top and bottom moldings; this is less expensive and makes a more subdued decorative statement. The product shown on these pages, also generally available at home centers, is made of molded fiberboard that is painted on one side. The bead-board pieces come already cut to length, and the top and bottom molding pieces have channels (or rabbets) into which the bead board fits easily.

Installing Bead-Board Wainscoting

• Stud finder • Level • Miter saw or power miter saw • Base and saw • Bead-board panels, pre-cut to about 3 feet long

1 Use a stud finder to locate studs. At a height that will be covered by the chair rail (Step 7), make a mark for each stud.

This wainscoting, at about 5 ft. above the floor, is taller than the usual chair-rail height and is capped by a narrow shelf for displaying decorative items.

4 Slip the first wainscoting board into the base molding and against the corner, and use a level to make it plumb. If there is a gap along the adjacent wall that is wider than ³/₈ in., scribe and cut it as shown in step 6. Apply two beads of adhesive to the wall, and attach the first piece by driving screws into the corner stud.

2 Measure and cut the baseboard pieces. If the wainscoting will turn an outside corner, make miter cuts for the corner. (The joints may not be perfect, but you may be able to file the backs of the miter cuts to fit the joints better or fill gaps with caulk. If the wainscoting turns an inside corner, use a coped cut instead.)

3 Attach the base molding with finishing nails or screws. Square-drive trimhead screws are ideal. In most cases you can drive fasteners into a framing base plate that runs all along the floor, so you don't have to locate studs.

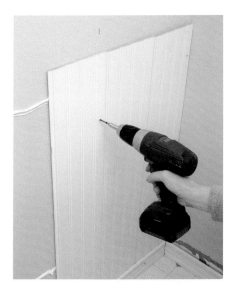

5 Place the next boards into the base molding channel, and press them into the adhesive. Test the adhesion by pulling a piece away; if it is not sticking, thicken the bead of adhesive. When you reach a stud, drive two or three screws or nails.

6 When you start wainscoting the adjacent wall, drive a temporary screw or two to hold the first board so it is plumb. If there is a gap along the length of the board, slide a scrap of wood and a pencil tip along the board to mark for a cut that will match the adjacent wall. Cut the board using a saber saw or circular saw.

7 Cut pieces of chair rail the same way you cut the base molding. Attach it by driving nails or screws into studs. Fill the fastener holes with vinyl spackle, and apply a bead of caulk along the corner if needed. Apply two coats of durable paint, such as 100 percent acrylic.

Window Treatments

Some people consider a window behind or near the shower or tub a liability—the worries about rot and mildew not being worth the aesthetic appeal. In many older homes, water may have infiltrated into the window's wood, rotting the trim and perhaps the framing as well. As a result, many of these windows have been removed and walled over or replaced with glass-block units.

But there are advantages to having a window in the bathroom. Natural sunlight makes a bathroom feel fresh and bright—and it beats artificial light for putting on makeup. Natural light, as well as ventilation provided by opening a window, can help disinfect and fight mildew. Then, of course, there's the decorative bonus. You can add a charming window treatment to tie the room together, and for company or just for a special treat, an occasional vase of flowers is charming on the windowsill.

For privacy, many people install frosted glass for their shower window or add a frosted film coating. (See page 161.) But your window treatment can also take care of privacy. Popular bathroom window treatments include shutters that open and close from the inside, blinds, and a variety of shades and curtains, including Roman shades. The trick is to choose a window treatment that can handle the moisture. For blinds, choose faux wood rather than real wood; for shades, vinyl is durable and is available in a variety of colors and patterns. For curtains, outdoor fabrics are one option; or cut a shower curtain to make panels and tie-backs.

Blinds are more commonly used in other rooms of the house, but they add a pleasant sense of formality in the bathroom. Most people choose synthetic materials to reduce problems with mold or warping. The Venetian blinds shown here let window light glow through while still maintaining privacy.

Interior shutters have a basic old-fashioned appeal, maybe even a little bit romantic. They provide flexible privacy and light control. The only drawback is that they can be difficult to clean or paint. Frequent vacuuming with the brush attachment is one way to keep them clean. If you need to paint them, spray paint is the easiest method. Though white is the traditional color for shutters, you can paint them any color you choose.

The boundaries between shades and blinds are a bit fuzzy these days. Some people would call this treatment a pleated blind or roller blind. Either way, it works like a shade, but it is more stylish than the plastic shades that were typical a decade or two ago. Colored shades glimmer when the sun shines through and brightens up the room.

Many people have a color phobia and avoid bold hues in their decorating scheme, but the nice thing about curtains is you can change them when you get tired of them, and it won't cost a lot. If your window treatment is the finishing touch for your bathroom, it's an opportunity for you to tie the room together by adding a splash of color or style—whatever the room seems to need. Exotic scarves or fabric pieces from foreign lands can spice things up and make you smile when you enter the room.

Obscure Glass

If the view out your bathroom window is less than appealing, or if you worry that neighbors can see in, then "obscure" glass may be the solution. You can replace plain glass panes with decorative glass that lets in the light but not the view. Simple obscure, or "frosted," glass blurs the view. You can also choose glass with a subtle floral pattern; one that mimics the look of raindrops on glass; or "seeded" glass, which is peppered with bubbles. Glass variously described with words like "cord" or "reed" uses vertical lines to achieve a sort of Deco look.

Obscure It Yourself

For a very small price and minimal effort you can apply window film onto glass. Though you may skeptically assume the resulting window will appear tacky, people are often surprised at and impressed by how well the result mimics patterned glass. Here we show installing a film with a "rice paper" pattern. You can also choose other obscure types, or even films with colorful stained-glass patterns.

Measure the glass you want to cover. Working on a flat surface, use a sharp utility knife, and a straightedge to cut the film to fit ❶. Clean the glass thoroughly. Fill a spray bottle with water, and add a few drops of liquid soap. Shake to mix, and spray the glass ❷. Starting in a corner, peel the film from its paper backing ❸. Handle the film carefully to keep from creasing it. Place the side that was paper-backed onto the wet glass ❹. You can adjust the film's position after placing it. Wet the front of the film. Starting from the center and working outward, use a squeegee to squeeze out all air bubbles ❺. Keep squeegeeing until the film is dry.

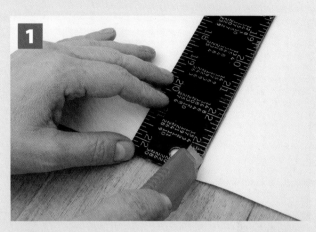

Bringing in the Light: Solar Tube

A solar tube (light tube, sun tunnel, sun tube, or tubular skylight) is a great way to bathe a bathroom in natural light. Best of all, in can be installed at a fraction of the expense of adding a skylight. The concept is simple: A transparent globe on the roof captures natural light and sends it, via a reflective tube, to a room below. The result can be so dramatic that you'll find yourself reaching for the light switch as you leave the room. A 10-inch solar tube, the smallest option, supplies the equivalent of three 100-watt bulbs, enough to illuminate up to 200 square feet of floor area. Larger 14-inch tubes can brighten as much as 300 square feet, providing the equivalent of five 100-watt bulbs.

A basic solar tube can be enhanced with options, including baffles powered by a rheostat or a hand-held remote, to tone down intense sunlight. A range of ceiling-mounted diffusers lets you choose between brilliant, soft, or warm light. For illumination after sunset, some manufacturers offer a tube-mounted bulb that can be switched on after dark.

Before purchasing a solar tube, check the attic space above. Measure from a ceiling-mounted bathroom vent fan to help determine the location of the solar tube when you are in the attic. Or drill a small hole in the ceiling, and push in a straightened coat hanger as a guide. Look for a clear path to the roof, bearing in mind that the tube can be installed at an angle. Some manufacturers offer flexible tubing to get around obstructions.

Running a solar tube from the roof to the first floor of a two-story house is feasible if you have a handy closet or mechanical chase through which you can run the tube. This will require some careful measuring. Be aware that you may encounter wiring, plumbing, or heating/air-conditioning ducts along the way.

A solar tube is an affordable way to bring natural light into a bathroom while maintaining privacy.

A Tube to Suit Any Space

A short, straight solar tube located on a roof with southern exposure provides the most light. Flexible tubing allows you to dodge obstructions. In either case, maximum recommended length is 20 feet.

Installing a Solar Tube

• Solar-tube kit • Drywall saw • Hammer • Measuring tape • Drill-driver • Reciprocating saw or saber saw • Roofing cement •
Trowel • Flashing, caulk • Roofing nails • Scissors

1 Trace the ceiling ring to mark a cut line, centering it on the protruding nail, or scribe a circle according to the manufacturer's specs. Cut a hole using a drywall saw or saber saw.

2 Install the ring. It comes with flanges that swing out to grip the ceiling from behind.

3 Up in the attic, select a location for the rooftop globe. At a point centered between two rafters, drive a large nail to mark the location of the hole. Use the flashing to mark for cutting a hole in the roof.

4 Drill a couple of ¾-in. access holes for sawing. With a reciprocating saw (shown) or a saber saw, cut the opening.

Continued on next page

Installing a Solar Tube, cont'd.

5 Check the manufacturer's instructions for cutting away roofing to install the flashing. Typically, the flashing overlaps only the bottom-most course of shingles. Otherwise, shingles should overlap the flashing. Pry out nearby roofing nails as needed. Trowel on roofing cement around the hole, and then slip the flashing in place.

6 Nail the flashing. Seal down adjacent shingles with roof cement or flashing caulk. Caulk any nailheads.

10 Assemble the entire tube, including the elbows. Use painter's tape for a trial assembly. Make a test-fit. Adjust the joints as needed; then permanently assemble the tube with screws and foil tape.

11 Lower the entire assembly into the roof. Have a helper ease the lower elbow of the assembly into the ceiling ring. Fasten the tube to the inner lip of the roof flashing using the screws provided.

12 Set the dome on the flashing, and line up the fastener holes. Secure the dome using the screws provided. Fasten the screws firmly, but don't overtighten them.

7 Add the pivot ring to the roof elbow. It may take some doing to push it past the joints of the elbow. Install the roof elbow in the flashing. In the attic, fit the lower elbow onto the ceiling ring.

8 Measure for the tube section, including the elbows, as recommended by the manufacturer.

9 Cut a tube section to length. Remove the protective film, and join the tube edges together using the double-sided tape provided on the tube section.

13 Indoors, secure the lower elbow to the ceiling ring using self-tapping screws.

14 Install the diffuser with the frosted or prismatic side down. Fasten it to the ceiling ring by rotating the plastic locks.

6
Electrical Upgrades

You may be (justifiably) frightened of electricity and leery of working on an electrical circuit panel. But many electrical improvements can be successfully handled by a careful homeowner. This chapter will give you cautious instructions for replacing a light fixture and a fan/light, replacing a standard receptacle with a ground-fault-circuit-interrupter (GFCI) receptacle, and installing a new set of mirror lights. You'll also learn how to install a wall-mounted heating unit as well as radiant heating

When working with electricity, there are three main safety rules you should follow: (1) shut off power before you work; (2) test to verify that power is off; and (3) take steps to ensure that power will not be turned on while you work.

In addition, it's important not to overload an electrical circuit. This is not an issue when you are replacing a light fixture or receptacle with another of the same type. But if you will install new services, like heating units, you will most likely need to install a new circuit. In that case, you may want to call in an electrician. See pages 214-19 for more information.

Choosing Lighting

Most bathrooms have two kinds of lighting: the first, ambient, or general, lighting, illuminates the entire room and is usually supplied by one or more ceiling fixtures; the second, task lighting, is directed at a specific area—in a bathroom, that almost always means the mirror or mirrored medicine cabinet above a lavatory.

Creatures of habit that we are, most of us are accustomed to our bathroom lighting and unaware of other possibilities. But increasing or redirecting the room's illumination can effect a dramatic improvement, making your bathroom brighter and livelier and lighting your face more fully when you look in the mirror.

Getting More Lighting without Adding Fixtures

Many bathrooms are under-lit. Chances are, you can greatly increase your lighting without running new cable and installing new electrical boxes for new fixtures.

You may have an inexpensive overhead light that is rated for only a single 60- or 75-watt lightbulb. If the fixture's globe is large enough, you can replace the incandescent bulbs with compact fluorescent lamps (CFLs), which supply more light for the wattage. For instance, a 23-watt CFL will supply the same amount of light as a 100-watt incandescent. LED bulbs are also an option, though a bit pricier.

You may choose to install a new fixture. As you can see from the instructions on pages 176-77, it's not a difficult job. Be sure to get one that will supply plenty of light. Many fixtures now come with compact fluorescent or other low-voltage bulbs. Check the lumens: 1,600 lumens is the same amount of light as that from a 100-watt incandescent lightbulb.

Some light fixtures have multiple lights mounted on a pole, which may be 2 to 4 feet long. Installing one is no more difficult than installing a standard fixture, but the fixture will allow you to direct light at various areas of the bathroom.

A hanging globe, four medicine cabinet sconces, and recessed canisters, opposite, are all part of the lighting team in this large bathroom.

Three globular pendants, above, add some colorful fun.

Not designed specifically for bathroom use, these sconces, right, add a nice living-room touch. They might not last long if the room gets damp from heavy shower use for prolonged periods, but in a powder room they would work just fine.

Lights by the Mirror

Experts say that the best light for applying makeup is natural light, but because that is often not available, the next-best option is to use bulbs that replicate a soft, warm natural light. This has traditionally been achieved through coated or lightly colored incandescent bulbs because conventional fluorescent tubes or bulbs cast an illumination that is too "cold," or blue-green in color. But nowadays you can buy CFLs and other low-voltage bulbs that have a "warmer" tone. Color temperature is measured by the Kelvin scale. For a look that mimics natural sunlight, choose bulbs that have a color temperature between 2,700 and 3,000 K.

For applying makeup, most experts say you should place a light on each side of the mirror at eye level. The main thing is to direct a soft and shadow-free light at the face and not the mirror. Shadows will tend to come from nearby overhead lights, like pendants or recessed lights positioned close enough to the mirror to create shadows. None of the face's features, such as the nose or eyes, should be in a shadow.

A dimming feature is also recommended for mirror lighting because you will apply makeup for an occasion that is dimly lit differently from one that is brightly lit, and facial makeup will turn out best if you can replicate the level of light in which you will be seen. But for applying eye makeup, it's best to use bright light to get the details right. A shielded fixture will reduce glare, but you can also use unadorned bulbs or crystal glass fixtures with a lower wattage to get good makeup lighting. Or consider a swing-arm vanity mirror with one side magnified for applying makeup.

At the same time, it's actually better to have light from above for shaving. So if your family needs a given mirror for both shaving and applying makeup, consider a scheme that has light from above as well as from the side but is controlled by independent switches.

Think of your bathroom lighting as a total system. The ambient (general) lighting supplied by an overhead fixture can have a great impact on mirror lighting. If your ambient lighting is bright and well diffused and does not create sharp shadows, then it will help your mirror lighting. If it points sharply at the back of your head, however, then the mirror lighting will have to be especially strong.

An oval wall mirror with an integral wraparound light, opposite top, is wired much like a light fixture.

Two widely spaced sconces, opposite bottom, will not effectively light up this mirror; well-positioned overhead lights must come to their aid.

Unique and sleek sconces, left, may be a bit pricy, but they make a memorable design statement, even alongside a straightforward medicine cabinet.

Unusual sconces that feature three lights each, bottom left, effectively brighten up a tall mirror, top to bottom.

Slightly ornate but certainly not gaudy, a pair of classic sconces, below, adds just the right old-fashioned touch in this bathroom.

Bathroom Sconces

Wall sconces flanking a bathroom mirror look stylish and provide ideal light for applying makeup and adequate light for shaving. Most importantly, they eliminate the harsh shadows an overhead fixture creates.

This project involves removing an over-the-mirror fixture and installing sconces. It requires some prep work. Begin by using a stud finder to determine stud locations. Mark for remodeling-type electrical boxes that will hold the sconces, positioning them about 36 inches apart and about 60 inches above the floor. Avoid locating a box where there is a stud. If you have no alternative, you'll have to cut and chisel the stud deeply enough to install the box and clear the stud.

Consult pages 214-19 for information on bathroom wiring and connecting techniques. Once you have your project laid out, shut off power at the breaker panel and remove the old light fixture. As you remove the fixture, have a helper support it or hang it from a bent clothes hanger while you disconnect the wires.

Once you complete your installation, you'll have to cover the old box. Never drywall over a junction box—to do so is a code violation and could create a potentially dangerous situation. Instead, add a paintable box cover as shown in Step 8, or cover the box with a standard metal cover and install a tall mirror over it.

Sleek sconces made of brushed chrome and frosted glass match the accompanying faucet and vessel sink in this contemporary bathroom.

BEFORE

AFTER

Sconces make a stylish addition to a bathroom. A flattering alternative to over-mirror lights, they provide balanced, even lighting without harsh shadows, ideal for applying makeup. See pages 174-175 for how to install sconces, step by step.

Installing Bathroom Sconces

• Stud finder and pencil • Remodeling-type electrical boxes • Drywall saw • Hole saw • Drill-driver • Carpenter's level
• Needle-nose pliers • Cable staples • Paintable or standard utility box cove • Drywall tape, compound (optional)

1 Cut a hole in the drywall large enough to bore holes through studs to get access to the boxes. Position the hole so that the mirror will cover it. That way, you won't have to worry about finessing the taping job and repainting.

2 Hold the face of a remodeling-type box against the wall. Trace around the box, allowing for the wings that will swing out as you install the box. A 3⅝-in. hole saw (shown) makes quick work of the job. Or cut using a drywall saw. In either case, use a drywall saw to cut notches for the wings.

5 Fasten strips of wood behind the drywall as a fastening surface for the drywall patch. Attach the patch using drywall screws. Because the mirror will cover the patch, taping the joints is optional.

6 A bracket or a strap and center fastening stud come with the wall sconce. Install it in the box with the fasteners provided. If necessary, use a torpedo level to align the bracket as you install it.

7 Use a bent wire clothes hanger to hold the fixture. Confirm that power is off. Connect the ground wires. Then splice the white wire to white, black to black. If you haven't relocated the power cable, connect the wires at the old box.

• 14/2 Electrical cable and cable clamps • Utility knife • Wire strippers • Wall sconces and wire clothes hanger • Torpedo level

3 Using a ¾-in. bit, bore holes in the centers of studs so you can run cable to the box holes. In some cases you maybe able to relocate the original power cable to one of your new boxes and run a second cable to the other box. Strip 6 in. of sheathing off of each cable. (See page 217.)

4 Feed the cable into each box until ½ in. of sheathing shows in the box. Push the box into the hole. Enlarge the notches as necessary—forcing the box can damage the drywall. Tighten the screws until you feel the wings grab the drywall from behind.

8 Add a paintable cover (shown) to disguise the original junction box. Or seal it off with a standard metal cover, and install a tall mirror.

9 Slip the sconce onto the bracket stud after carefully folding all of the wires into the electrical box, and fasten the fixture in place. Check that no wires are caught as you do so. Add lightbulbs; restore power; and test your installation.

Ceiling Light

Though it may seem like a permanent part of your house, a ceiling light fixture is usually easy to remove and replace. Most new fixtures come with mounting hardware (usually, a strap with screws) that attaches easily to a standard electrical box. In many cases, you can simply reuse the mounting hardware from the old fixture. If you live in an older home with a thin "pancake" box that uses different hardware, take a photo of the box and show it to an electrical salesperson, who can to help you choose adapter hardware pieces.

If possible, choose a new fixture with a canopy (the part that snugs up to the ceiling) that is at least as wide as the old one. If it is smaller, you may need to patch and paint the exposed portion of the ceiling.

Depending on your wiring, there may still be power present in the box even with the light switch turned off. See pages pages 214—15 for full instructions on shutting off power and verifying that power is off.

A ceiling light in a moist location should have a watertight lens; many fixtures have this feature.

Replacing a Ceiling Light

• Screwdriver or drill with screwdriver bit • Voltage tester

1 Shut off power to the circuit at your service electrical panel, and test that power is off by turning on the switch. Working on a non-metallic ladder, loosen the screws holding the globe onto the canopy, and remove the globe.

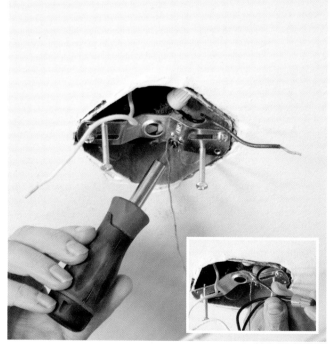

4 Loosen the green grounding screw; wrap the end of the (bare) grounding wire around it; and tighten the screw. Use wire connectors to splice the black house wire to the black lead (inset) and the white wire to the white lead. Tug to make sure that the connections are firm.

• Wire strippers • New ceiling light with mounting hardware

2 Loosen or remove the mounting screws that hold the canopy. (If the fixture is center-mounted, unscrew the mounting nut in the center of the canopy.) Gently pull the canopy down; spread the two wires apart; and remove the wire connectors (inset).

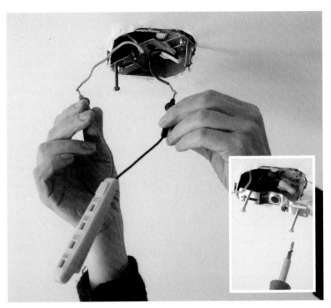

3 To make sure power is off, touch the probes of a voltage tester to the two bare wire ends; then touch the end of the black or colored wire and the ground wire or the box if it is metal. No voltage should register. Attach the new strap to the box by driving two screws (inset).

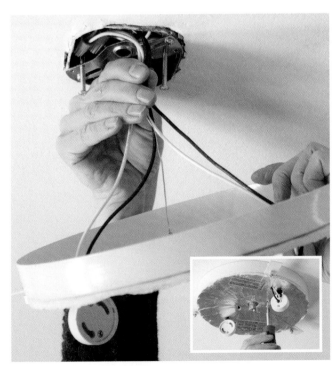

5 Fold the wires up into the box so that the connections will be inside the box rather than against the ceiling. Thread the mounting screws through the holes in the canopy, and tighten them to firmly attach the canopy to the ceiling (inset).

6 Assemble the parts of the globe, if necessary, and attach the globe to the canopy. This globe attaches via a center rod and nut; other globes attach using three outer screws, as seen in Step 1.

177

Ventilating Fan

A ventilating, or exhaust, fan removes water vapor from a bathroom, making the bathroom more pleasant and reducing mold. If you have a fan that is not venting well enough, replace it with a stronger one; fix the ductwork; or install an additional fan.

Some units include a light, a nightlight, and even a heating unit. (A heating unit uses a good deal of power, which may require running a new electrical circuit.) To install a fan-only unit or one that turns the fan on at the same time as the light, run two-wire cable from the switch to the fan. For a unit with a light that comes on separately,

consult manufacturer's instructions; you may need three-wire cable or two sets of cable.

Pages 180–81 show running ducts to a roof vent. However, if it is more accessible, you may choose to run the duct straight out an exterior wall or snake it along the attic floor and down through an eave or soffit. Use a wall vent or a soffit vent, respectively.

Once you have installed a fan, you simply snap the plastic canopy in place. Clean it once a year or so to maintain good airflow.

Duct Locations

Running the vent from a bathroom exhaust fan to the outside can take some creativity. The most direct route is usually straight up through the roof. But the one that is most protected from the weather is running the duct between ceiling joists and out through the soffit.

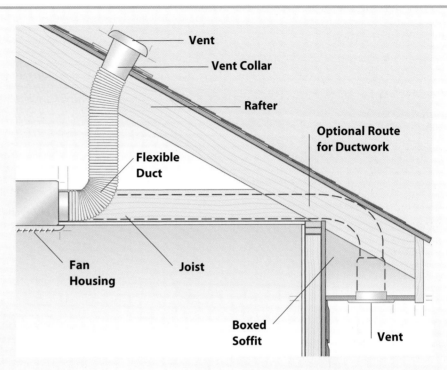

Vent
Vent Collar
Rafter
Optional Route for Ductwork
Flexible Duct
Fan Housing
Joist
Boxed Soffit
Vent

Match the Fan to the Job

TIP

To choose a fan that will expel moisture effectively or to address a problem with an existing fan that is not doing the job, consider both the fan and the ductwork.

- See that the fan is strong enough for the room's volume. Ventilating fans are sized by the number of cubic feet of air they move per minute (cfm). To choose a fan that is adequate for the job, find the room's volume: multiply its length times its width times its height. Then divide the volume by 7.5. For example, if a bathroom is 7 feet by 8 feet with an 8-foot-high ceiling, its volume is 448 cubic inches (7 x 8 x 8 = 448). Divide 448 by 7.5 to get about 60, and buy a fan that has an air-handling rating greater than 60 cfm.
- Ducts leading from the fan to the outside must be tightly connected and free of obstructions. Cheap plastic ribbed ductwork is not as efficient as the metal ductwork shown on page 180, so if you have plastic ductwork, replacing it may help your fan work more efficiently. Ductwork that takes a meandering path will be less efficient than that which makes minimal turns. If a duct must be longer than 6 feet, buy a stronger fan.

You Need to Vent

Because venting an exhaust fan can be difficult, it's tempting to omit the duct altogether and just vent the exhaust fan into the attic space. No building codes permit this and their motivation isn't based on an excess of caution. By dumping large amounts of water vapor into the attic, you virtually ensure that water will condense out of the vapor and coat the framing members. This greatly increases the likelihood of serious damage cause by rot.

Installing a Ventilating Fan with Roof Vent

• Ventilating fan, wire, pencil • Drill-driver • Reciprocating, drywall, or saber saw • Screws • Solid and flexible ducts, with clamps • Vent

1 Decide on the approximate location of the fan on the ceiling. Drill a small hole, and feed a coat-hanger wire up through the ceiling and through any insulation.

2 Pull back insulation in the attic to find the reference wire. Establish the fan location. It should be installed against a framing member on one side. Drill small holes down through the ceiling at the corners of the fan.

5 From above, place the fan housing over the ceiling hole, and screw it to a framing member. Choose the most direct path for the vent duct, and attach it to the end of the fan housing using a screw clamp.

6 Extend the duct to the point where it goes through the roof or wall. Attach a solid vent collar to the end of the duct by driving self-tapping screws, then wrapping it with duct tape.

collar and cap for roof • Duct tape • Hammer • Caulk gun and silicone or roofing caulk • Electrical cable and switch box, with connectors

3 Press the fan housing against the ceiling so that its corners fall within the four reference holes. Trace around the housing to mark for the cut.

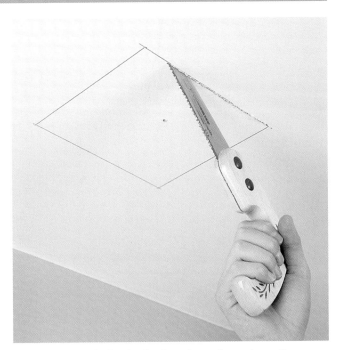

4 Cut the hole for the fan housing using a drywall saw, saber saw, or keyhole saw (shown).

7 Drill a locator hole up through the roof. Mark and cut a vent hole through the roof using a saber (shown) or reciprocating saw.

8 Pull the duct up through the hole. Carefully cut away shingles so they cover at least the upper half of the hood's flange, and attach and slip the hood in. Seal shingles using roof cement.

181

GFCI Receptacle

Bathrooms are moist places, which increases the chances of electrical shock. Ordinary grounded receptacles offer some protection against shock, but a ground-fault-circuit-interrupter (GFCI) receptacle offers much greater protection. In normal operation, power runs to the receptacle (and hence to any appliance plugged into the receptacle) via a black or colored "hot" wire, and returns from it via the white "neutral" wire. If a portion of the return current is missing—which could be caused by a person receiving a shock—a GFCI senses this "fault" and cuts off the power in about $\frac{1}{25}$th of a second.

Local and national electrical codes require that GFCI receptacles be installed in areas that could get wet—near a sink, for instance. Even if code does not demand it, it makes good sense to GFCI-protect all the receptacles in a bathroom. To do this, you can replace all the receptacles with GFCIs, or you may be able to install the first receptacle in a series in such a way as to protect the other receptacles down the line. Lights and fans near a tub or shower also should be GFCI protected, by installing a GFCI circuit breaker on the circuit.

GFCIs do not last forever. Test yours every month or so by pressing the TEST button; that should shut off power, and power should be restored when you press the RESET button. If the receptacle fails that test or simply stops supplying power, replace it with a new GFCI receptacle.

Which Wires are Incoming and Outgoing?

If there are four wires attaching to the receptacle, the incoming pair brings power and the outgoing pair carries power down the line to other receptacles or lights. To tell which ones are incoming, carefully separate the wires so that they cannot touch each other. Restore power, and touch the bare wire ends with a voltage tester. When you touch the black and white incoming wires, the tester light will glow. Shut off power, and attach the incoming wires to the LINE terminals.

Replacing a Receptacle with a GFCI

• Voltage tester • Screwdriver • Wire connectors

1 Turn off power to the circuit at the service panel. (See pages 214-19.) Insert the prongs of a voltage tester into the slots of the receptacle to make sure that power is off. If the indicator light comes on, you turned off the wrong circuit.

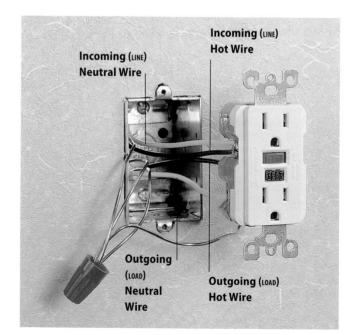

Incoming (LINE) Neutral Wire

Incoming (LINE) Hot Wire

Outgoing (LOAD) Neutral Wire

Outgoing (LOAD) Hot Wire

3 For tips on connecting to terminals, see page 216. Connect the grounding wire to the grounding terminal. Join the incoming hot (black) and neutral (white) wires to the terminals marked LINE. If outgoing wires are present, connect these to the LOAD terminals.

• GFCI receptacle(s)

2 Remove the cover plate, and double-check for power by touching tester prongs to the black and white wires. Unscrew the receptacle's mounting screws; pull out the receptacle; and loosen or remove the terminal screws to free the wires. Remove the grounding wire. If the insulation or the bare wires are nicked, cut them and re-strip the ends.

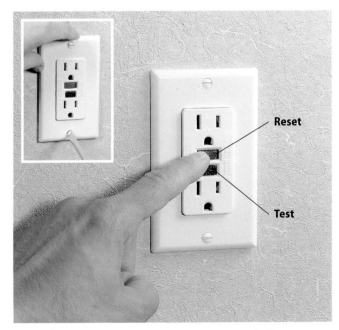

Reset

Test

4 Carefully fold the wires back in as you push the GFCI receptacle into the box and screw it in place. Attach the cover plate (inset). Turn on the power, and press the RESET button, then the TEST button. If the GFCI is working properly, the RESET button should pop out.

Circuit Breakers

Lights and fans in moist areas should be GFCI protected, and many codes require that all the circuits supplying a bathroom be GFCI protected. Do this by installing a GFCI circuit breaker or hiring an electrician to do so. The breaker is installed into the electrical service panel in the same way as a standard breaker, and the hot circuit wire is connected to it. Then the white corkscrew sire is attached to the neutral bus bar in the panel.

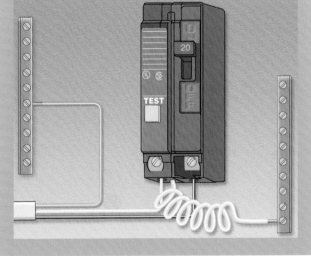

Will It Fit?

TIP

A GFCI receptacle is bulkier than a standard one, and you may have trouble fitting it into a small electrical box. If you find yourself having to really cram things in, call in an electrician; you may need a new, larger box.

183

Wall-Mounted Heater

If your bathroom is a little on the cool side during the winter, consider installing a small recessed wall heater. It will come with a white or off-white front grill that blends with most decors. Position it away from obstructions and hanging towels, so the warm air can circulate.

Some models are controlled by a separate switch/thermostat, which calls for additional wiring. The project on page 185 shows a model with a dial thermostat that's mounted on the front of the grill.

A wall-mounted heater is preferable to a combination ceiling unit, which includes fan, light, and heater, because it places the heat closer to the floor and can be controlled by a thermostat.

During the winter, it's an added comfort to have an extra-warm bathroom when you or your guests step out of the shower. A wall-mounted heater is just the ticket for that added boost of heat. It keeps your best friend happy, too.

Check the Wattage

A small heater may pull as few as 500 watts, while larger heaters use 2,000 watts or more. Consult page 215 to determine whether you can tap into an existing electrical receptacle in the bathroom without overloading its circuit or you need to put the heater on its own circuit. A 1,000-watt unit, for instance, uses over 8 amps, more than half the capacity of a 15-amp circuit; so unless there are only a couple of lights on that circuit, adding a heater will likely overload it.

If you need a new circuit, you must run cable to the electrical service panel, which may be simple if the bathroom is one floor above the room with the service panel but more difficult if you need to run the cable through multiple floors. If you are at all unsure about tapping safely into power, hire an electrician to do it for you.

Consider a Larger Heater

If your bathroom is quite cold and you are hiring a pro to install a heater anyway, it probably makes sense to have him install a larger-capacity 240-volt heater, which will operate more efficiently than a 120-volt unit. The cost of the unit should be only $100 or so greater, and you will not have to worry about running low on heat.

Installing a Wall-Mounted Heater

• Drywall saw • Cable and clamp • Wall heater • Screwdriver • Wire strippers • Drill-driver • Wire connectors

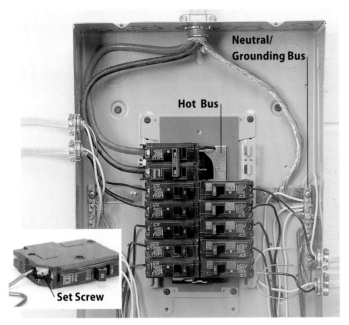

1 Determine how you will run the cable and attach to power. If you need to connect to a new circuit, see pages 218—19. Run the cable into the electrical service panel; connect it to a new circuit breaker; and snap the breaker onto the bus bars. Leave the circuit breaker turned off while you work.

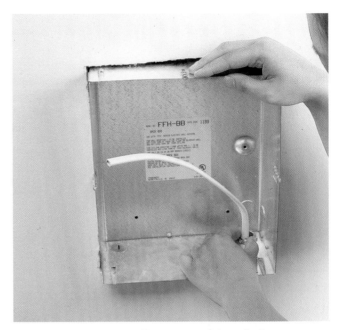

2 Cut a hole in the wall to accommodate the heater so that one side of the hole is alongside a stud. Run cable into this opening. Connect the cable to the heater housing using a cable clamp; allow for plenty of cable inside the housing. Push the housing into the wall.

3 Attach the housing so that its front edge is flush with the wall surface, by driving screws into the stud. Strip the cable sheathing and the wire insulation. Slide the heater into the housing, feeding the cable wires into the electrical box on the front of the heater.

4 Splice the cable wires to the heater wires using wire connectors. Splice white to white, black to black (or colored), and the grounding wire to the green grounding screw. Mount the grill over the wires (inset). Restore power, and test the unit.

Radiant Heat

Adding a new tile floor to your bath (next chapter) offers the opportunity to install the affordable luxury of electric radiant heat. With it, you'll be able to step out of the shower onto a toasty warm floor. The heat comes from a mat embedded under the tile. A wall-mounted thermostat and timer control heating wires woven into the mat. The timer allows you to use the radiant heat only when you need it. It warms up in advance and shuts off thermostatically.

In most of the country electric heat is fairly expensive, but when you consider that bathroom floor space is small—and this excludes vanity, tub, and toilet areas, which would not require radiant wiring—it usually will not increase a utility bill that much. Hot-water radiant heat, usually connected to a gas-fired boiler, is also available, but a professional should perform the installation.

Begin by planning the location of the mats. They should be 3 inches away from walls and 4–6 inches from toilet rings. Locate mats only in the areas where they are needed—not under a vanity, for example. Measure your bathroom; draw a floor plan; and plan your layout precisely. This can be challenging because you must use whole mats; they cannot be trimmed in any way that cuts through a heating wire.

Handle the mats carefully, making sure that the wires are never crimped or nicked. Test them frequently with an ohmmeter (Step 2). Damaged heating wires cannot be repaired.

The mats shown here pull only 1.5 amps—less power than that of two 100-watt lightbulbs—so it is unlikely you would overload a circuit by plugging them in. To be certain, or if you plan a large installation, see pages 218—19. The receptacle should be GFCI protected. (See pages 182–83.) Read the manufacturer's requirements carefully.

Radiant heat warms you, not the air. Combined with ceramic tile, it is ideal for a bathroom. By means of a thermostat/timer, the floor can be warm when you need it and turned down when you don't.

Installing a Radiant Heater

• Single-gang, deep box • GFCI receptacle • 14/2 or 12/2 cable (12/3 for 240-volt installations) • Wire connectors • Digital ohmmeter • Wire strippers • Cutting pliers • Scissors • Hot glue gun • Painters' tape • Electrician's fish tape or a weighted string • Self-leveling cement • Tile and tile-setting tools and materials • Eye protection

1 Using a drywall saw, cut a hole for the thermostat/timer box 60 in. above the floor. Plan to tap power from a nearby outlet. If the receptacle is not GFCI protected, see pages 182–83 for installing one. Plan to connect the wires for the radiant heat to the receptacle's LOAD terminals. Run cable to the source, but do not connect it yet.

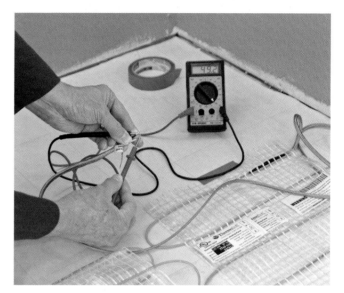

2 As soon as you take the mats out of the box and periodically as you install them, use a digital ohmmeter to check that the heating wires have not been damaged. Look for a reading within 10 percent of the rating you'll find handwritten on the UL (Underwriter's Laboratory) label.

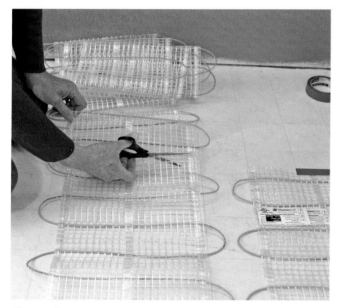

3 Each mat comes with a 10-ft.-long connecting lead. Do a dry run, positioning the mats so that their leads can be fished up a wall to the thermostat/timer. The fiberglass mat can be cut with a scissors as needed, as long as you do not cut any heating wire.

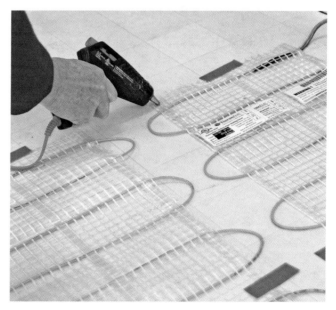

4 Once you've laid out the mat, adhere it to the floor using hot glue or tape. Be careful to fasten the mat so it is completely flat.

Continued on next page

Installing a Radiant Heater, cont'd.

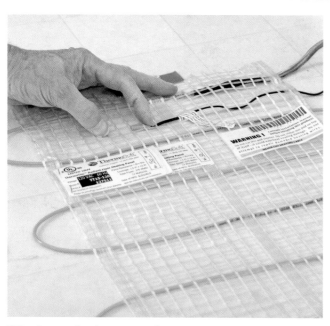

5 Center the thermostat floor sensor between two heating wires. If necessary, notch the subfloor to nest the sensor probe so that tiles will lay flat. Weave the sensor through the heating-mat mesh to hold it in place.

6 Using an electrician's fish tape or a weighted string, pull the lead and the sensor wires through the wall cavity and up to the opening for thermostat/timer box.

8 Apply a layer of self-leveling cement (shown) or thinset to cover the mesh. If you're applying thinset, use a plastic trowel to avoid nicking the heating wires. Be careful not to snag the mesh. Let the layer dry.

9 Once the covering layer has dried, apply thinset using a notched trowel as recommended by the tile manufacturer. Apply the tile and grout.

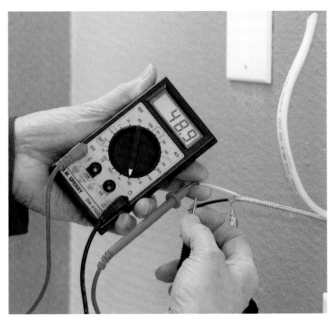

7 At the box, check the leads' resistance using the ohm-meter to ensure that no heating wires have been damaged during installation.

10 Attach the incoming power wires to the LINE terminals. Attach the mat leads to the LOAD terminals. Connect the wires from the floor sensor to the terminals marked SENSOR. Lastly, be sure to shut off power at the service panel, and make the connection to the power source. Follow the manufacturer's instructions for setting the time and temperature.

Towel Warmers

The luxury of a toasty-warm towel after a shower or bath is easy to achieve using a towel warmer. An electric towel warmer takes no more wall space than a towel rack, and simply plugs into the wall. A typical warmer heats slowly, so it usually runs continuously; it uses less energy than a 100-watt lightbulb. You can also use it to dry delicate clothing items.

7
Flooring

A bathroom floor needs to repel water effectively, but fortunately that doesn't limit design options. As the following four pages show, there are plenty of beautiful products from which to choose. This chapter concentrates on the most popular tile and sheet products. A motivated homeowner can install any of these products using inexpensive tools. (For cutting hard tile or stone, you will likely need to rent a wet-cutting tile saw.) Look through the projects to get an idea of the work involved. Bathroom floors are usually small, which limits the heavy lifting. If you have a weak back, however, you may want to hire a contractor to avoid the possibility of straining it from repetitive kneeling down and getting up. If you are removing your flooring to install new flooring, you may want to take the opportunity to install radiant floor heat (pages 186-89). Your new floor will be as comfortable as it is pretty!

Flooring Options

Unless it is only lightly used, expect your bathroom floor to get wet on a regular basis. The flooring you install should effectively resist water; it should be easy to clean; and it should be skid resistant. There are numerous products that meet these criteria. These four pages show some of the most popular.

Plan the floor along with the wall. Many people like the seamless look created by floor and wall tiles of the same or similar materials. If your walls will be painted, take a sample tile in with you to choose a paint that picks up one of its colors or contrasts with it pleasantly.

Before you shop, measure your bathroom and make a scale drawing to show to a flooring salesperson; this will make it easy to select the right amount of materials. Consult pages 196-97 as well as the installation instructions for your kind of flooring to choose the right subsurface materials so that the new flooring will rest on a solid-enough surface and will not be more than ½ inch higher than any adjacent flooring surface.

These days, some brave souls install wood, bamboo, or cork flooring in bathrooms. Such materials can work as long as they are kept well sealed and the floor does not get very wet. But ceramic or stone tile and vinyl tile or sheet flooring are considered more practical.

The Stone Look

Floors with earthy colors that look like natural stone used to be uncommon in bathrooms but have become popular in recent years. You can achieve this look by installing actual stone tile, or you can use ceramic or porcelain tile that mimics the look of the real thing. The faux products will usually be easier to maintain and keep clean.

Ceramic Tile. Ceramic tile comes in a dizzying array of colors, sizes, and shapes—and just as large a variety of prices. Be sure to choose "floor tile"; many tiles made for walls are too fragile to bear much weight and will eventually crack if applied to a floor. Different ceramic tiles have very different characteristics.

The Importance of Grout

Stone and ceramic tiles are to varying degrees water and stain resistant, but all of them have grout lines, which can be the weak link. Be sure to choose a grout that is latex or polymer fortified. Because floor tiles almost always have grout lines at least ⅛ inch wide, you should use sanded grout, which is stronger than unsanded varieties. It's also important to take a few minutes every 6 months or so to apply grout sealer to the joints.

Large ceramic tiles (16 in. sq.) with swirl patterns have colors that match two of the wall tile colors, which helps tie together a natural-looking floor and a geometric-patterned wall.

An old-fashioned cross-shaped mosaic pattern in a dreamy shade of blue, left, feels comfortably at home with surrounding marble tiles.

Solid tongue-and-groove wood flooring in a herringbone pattern, right, needs to be kept well sealed.

Dark mosaics, borders, sink, and woodwork, right, make this bathroom seem like a grotto hideaway.

- **Glazed ceramic tile.** Tiles with a hard-baked glossy, matte, or textured surface offer the greatest resistance to moisture and stains. Glazed tiles come in bright colors, pastels, or earth tones. In a bathroom, high-gloss glazing for a floor is not a good idea because it is slippery even when it's not wet—unless the tiles are 4 in. or smaller, in which case the grout lines will add skid resistance. Matte glazing is less slippery, and textured glazed tiles are the most slip-resistant.

- **Quarry tile.** Unglazed ceramic tiles are often called quarry tiles, though they are not cut from a quarry. Colors generally run from grays to earth tones. Quarry tiles offer good slip resistance and keep water from penetrating to the subfloor, but they are porous, so they are somewhat susceptible to staining. For that reason, they need to be sealed regularly.

- **Porcelain tile.** Made by firing at very high temperatures, porcelain tiles are extremely strong and stain resistant. Because of their strength, they are usually thinner than standard ceramics, which may help keep a floor from being too high in relation to adjacent floors. They are available in just about any size, color, and texture. Some porcelain tiles are nearly indistinguishable from travertine, marble, and other natural stone.

- **Mosaic tile.** Mosaics usually come in mesh-backed 12-inch-square sheets that contain a number of individual tiles ranging in size from 1 to 4 inches. Installation can be a bit tricky. The thinset mortar must be just the right thickness and consistency, or it can either ooze out onto the top of the tiles or not stick to all of the tiles. But the sheets are easy to cut, and grouting is not difficult.

Natural Stone. Real stone has a distinguished, one-of-a-kind appeal that many people feel can't be duplicated by glazed ceramic or porcelain products.

- **Travertine and smooth granite and marble.** Glossy 12-inch-square tiles made of granite are extremely moisture and stain resistant, but they can be a bit slippery. There are many possible colors and patterns that range from speckled to veined. Marble has beautiful veined patterns, but because it stains easily, it must be sealed regularly. Travertine boasts wonderful earth-toned hues, but like marble, it is not stain-resistant.
- **Slate.** This stone is sliced rather than cut, resulting in a texture that is wavy but not rough, so it feels pleasant on the feet and is slip resistant. The least expensive slate tiles tend to be soft and prone to flaking, making them practical only on walls. Other types are quite strong but need to be sealed regularly.
- **Rough-surface stone.** Tiles made of marble, granite, or other stone and described with words like "honed" or "sandblasted" have a softer appearance and may have tiny surface holes and pits. Some have rounded-over

Slate tiles on a bathroom floor, opposite top, show off the many colors, patterns, and textures that this natural stone can achieve. Joints are kept to $1/8$ in. to better display the tiles.

This medallion, opposite bottom, comes in an easy-to-install ensemble, but the surrounding tiles must be curve-cut precisely.

High-end vinyl tiles, right, have stone-like texture and edges that artfully mimic the look of grout lines.

Bright aqua-blue mosaic ceramic tiles, right, shine beautifully; the many grout lines help traction when the tiles get wet.

edges as well. Many of these tiles are available in decorative ensembles that include borders and accent tiles. The tiles feel comfortable underfoot, but as you may expect, you need to seal them regularly to protect them against staining.

Vinyl Tile and Sheet Flooring

Vinyl or vinyl composition tiles are commonly used in kitchens but are less popular in bathrooms. Vinyl sheet flooring, on the other hand, is often used in bathrooms. Erroneously called "linoleum" (an organic flooring material made from solidified linseed oil), vinyl sheet flooring has embossed surfaces for skid resistance. For some people vinyl has a less-than-stylish reputation, especially when they recall patterns from bygone decades that attempted to imitate ceramic tile or brickwork. But newer vinyl sheet products are worth considering; colors and patterns have improved in quality and have an understated appeal. Because they are continuous sheets, there are no grout lines and few if any seams where water can penetrate. Vinyl is inexpensive and can be installed quickly, but take care: a single cutting mistake can compromise the job.

Preparing for a Ceramic- or Stone-Tile Floor

The framing, plywood, and backer board that lie beneath the tiles are as important as the flooring itself. While sheet vinyl, wood strips, and other resilient flooring can be installed over a plywood subfloor that has some flex, a rigid-tile-floor substrate must be rock solid. Otherwise, the grout or even the tiles themselves can crack over time.

Strong-Enough Subfloor

To support ceramic or stone tiles, a floor should feel firm when a large adult jumps on it. The most common way to firm up the subfloor is with ¾-inch plywood topped by ½-inch concrete or fiber-cement backer board. Chances are that you already have the plywood, so you may need only to install the backer board.

If you suspect that your joists are weak or if you see signs of wood-eating insects, call in a professional carpenter or exterminator to examine the structure.

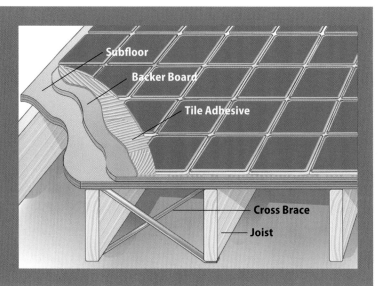

The Right Height and Graceful Transitions

If the new bathroom floor is ½ inch or more higher than an adjacent floor, such as in a hallway or living room, after you install backer board and tiles, then you will have what many people consider an awkward step up into the bathroom. In that case, you may want to choose porcelain tiles, which are thinner than ceramic or stone tiles. Or you may need to remove a layer or two of existing flooring—or go with another type of flooring.

Step-ups of ½ inch or less can be gracefully handled using transition strips, or thresholds. Transition strips are available to handle most situations, including the transition to a wood or carpeted floor. Inexpensive metal strips that overlay the joint are the easiest to cut and install, but they are unattractive and may create a tripping hazard. Strips that do not overlay the flooring (like the ones shown below) require precise cutting of the flooring but are far better looking than overlay types and make for a smoother transition.

Wooden Threshold

Marble Threshold

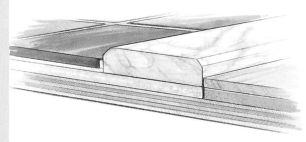

Removing Obstructions

It's almost always a bad idea to tile around a toilet, vanity, or other obstruction. It will make for a neater job and save you time in the long run if you temporarily remove the obstructions before you tile.

For the toilet, shut off the stop valve; disconnect the supply line and hold-down bolts; and remove it. (See pages 74-75.) **❶**. At the walls, pry away the base shoe and perhaps the base molding as well **❷**. If the trimwork pieces look to be in good shape, number their backs and remove any nails that may be stuck in them so that you can reinstall them later. If they look even a little ugly or worse for wear, replace them. Also remove a pedestal or vanity sink.

Laying out for angled tiles calls for careful planning. Here, full-size triangles are placed along the most visible wall.

Going over Existing Flooring?

TIP

You can install backer board directly on top of existing vinyl, wood, or other non-masonry-based flooring, as long as doing so will not make the new floor too high. You should remove ceramic or stone tiles using a flooring scraper.

Strengthening a Floor

Backer board will add some strength, but the plywood subsurface should feel pretty solid before you install it. If things feel bouncy, you may be able to strengthen the floor.

First try pulling out any loose nails; then drive screws through the subflooring and into joists below ❶. Drive screws every 10 inches in the middle of a sheet and every 6 inches around the perimeter. If the ceiling below is unfinished, you can check the joists. Hold a 4-foot level on the bottom of the joists to see whether any of them sag ❷. If a joist sags more than ½ inch, reinforce it. To strengthen a weak joist, cut a "sister" piece out of the same 2-by lumber as the joist, 6 feet or longer. Prop the sagging joist by wedging a 4x4 up against it or by using a flooring jack. Attach the sister to the sagging joist with a grid of 2 ½-inch screws ❸.

Checking for Level and Square

To see whether a floor is level or not, place a 4-foot level on a long, straight 2x4 ❶. If the floor is more than ½ inch out of level in a 10-foot span, it will be noticeable where the wall or cabinets meet the floor. Set some pieces of the finished floor in place to see if you can live with the discrepancy. If not, pull up the subflooring and install shims on top of joists to bring the flooring up to level.

Many bathroom floors are out of square, especially in older homes. An out-of-square condition can lead to a wedge-shaped row of tiles that increase in size. Check that the corners are square before you lay out the floor. Lay a sheet of plywood with two factory edges against a corner. Or use the 3-4-5 method: Measure from a corner along one wall to the 3-foot point, and mark the floor. Make a similar mark along the other wall at 4 feet. If the diagonal distance between the two marks is 5 feet, the room is square. If the corner is out of square, make your layout lines correspond with a square line rather than with the wall ❷.

Installing Backer Board

• Backer board • Backer-board scoring tool or utility knife • Thinset mortar • Fiber mesh tape • Backer-board screws
• Trowel with a flat side

1 Mark the panel for the cut. Score the line using a utility knife or backer-board scoring tool. It's easiest to score the first line with the board lying on the floor. Break the panel against your knee or over a piece of scrap placed on the floor.

2 Place the panel on edge; bend the panel back; and slice through the fiberglass mesh from the back of the cut. The cut edge will likely not be smooth; you may have to clean up the cut a bit.

3 For cutouts and notches, drill a starter hole; then cut using a saber saw equipped with a heavy-duty or tile blade.

4 Trowel mortar onto the floor, and set the panels in the mortar. Drive backer-board screws (not drywall screws, which are difficult to embed) in an 8-in. grid.

Laying a Ceramic-Tile Floor

A new tile floor can really brighten and class-up a bathroom floor. Because the floor is likely to be small, you may be able to afford high-end tiles. See pages 192-95 for descriptions of tile options.

Buy floor tiles; tiles made for walls will crack. Ask a salesperson to help you choose the spacers, which determine the width of the grout lines (usually at least $\frac{1}{8}$ inch; $\frac{3}{16}$ inch is one of the most popular). Select a grout color that harmonizes with the tiles. Fortified thinset mortar is almost always the best adhesive choice; pre-mixed mastic is easier to work with but not as resistant to moisture. If the tiles are light in color or even slightly translucent, use white rather than gray thinset. Buy a trowel with a notch size recommended for your tile; $\frac{1}{4}$-inch notches work for most applications, but if you have large or irregular tiles, you may need a trowel with $\frac{3}{8}$- or $\frac{1}{2}$-inch notches.

As long as you have the right tools for cutting the tiles of your choice, laying a ceramic-tile floor calls for no special skills—just careful planning and attention to detail. Preparation is vital, so follow the steps on pages 196-99 to make sure your floor is solid; check it for square; remove the toilet and other obstructions; and install backer board. It's also a good idea to install a threshold at the doorway, so account for that.

Tiles laid in straight rows with grout lines that are consistent in width make for an orderly and peaceful setting.

Laying Out

In a bathroom, the most visible line is usually where the floor meets the tub, so you will likely start your layout there. As long as the room is fairly square, you can use the simple layout method shown in Steps 1 through 3 on the next page. If the room is large or out of square, you may need to spend more time on the layout.

Use the 3-4-5 method (page 198) to snap two centerlines that are square to each other, as shown in the illustration at right. If laying the tiles against these lines will produce an unattractive row of narrow tiles, adjust one or both lines one-half of a tile's width.

To lay out for tiles at a diagonal, snap the centerlines. From the center point, measure out an equal distance along two adjacent lines, marked points A and B on the illustration. Tack a nail at these points. Hook the end of a measuring tape to one of the nails, and hold a pencil against the tape at a distance equal to that between the nail and the center point. Use the tape and pencil as a compass to scribe an arc on the floor. Repeat for the other nail, creating a second arc. The arcs intersect

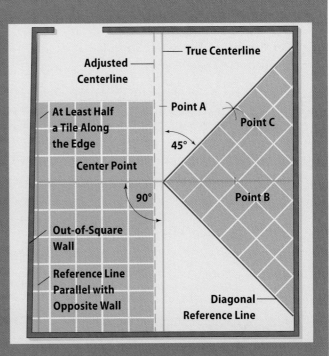

at point C. Snap a diagonal chalk line from the center point through point C. Repeat the process for the rest of the room.

Installing a Ceramic-Tile Floor

• Knee pads and protective eyewear • Chalk-line box • Partial sheet of plywood or other sheeting, for laying out • Floor tiles • Plastic spacers • Wet-cutting tile saw, snap cutter, or other tools needed to cut your tiles • Notched trowel • Fortified thinset mortar and mixing materials • Level, straight board, hammer • Fortified sanded grout and mixing materials • Grout float and large sponge • Caulk to match the grout color

1 Starting at the most conspicuous line visually (here, at the tub), lay tiles in a dry run, with spacers between them. Aim for a layout with large cut tiles at the walls that will be visible. Adjust one way or the other if you end up with a row of narrow tiles.

2 At one of the grout lines determined in Step 1, use a sheet of plywood, drywall, or (as shown here) backer board with two factory edges to create a perfectly square line. Draw along the edge of the sheet; then snap a chalk line to extend that line.

Continued on next page

Installing a Ceramic-Tile Floor, cont'd.

3 Also draw a perpendicular layout line, 2 or 3 ft. away from the tub or wall (so you can reach across it while setting tiles). Hold the sheet against the first line, and mark the floor at each end of the sheet; then snap a chalk line that extends across the room.

4 Cut a number of tiles that will go against the wall. In most cases, the cut ends will be covered by base shoe or other molding, so they can be ¼ in. short. Take into account the width of the grout lines when you measure. Using a snap cutter with a guide, you can easily cut a number of tiles to the same width.

Making a Curved Cut

Some floor tiles can be curve-cut using a saber saw with a tile-cutting blade, as shown on page 70.

For tougher-to-cut tiles or long cuts that may tax a saber-saw blade too much, use a wet-cutting tile saw. First, make a series of closely spaced cuts that run to the cut line ❶. Tap the resulting little fingers out with a hammer ❷. Use the saw's blade to scrape along the curved cut and remove any small protrusions ❸.

5 You can mix small amounts of thinset using a margin trowel. (See page 138.) For larger amounts, pour about 1 in. of water into a 5-gal. bucket; then scoop in some thinset. Mix using a drill equipped with a mixing paddle; hold the bucket still with your feet to keep it from spinning. Mix to the consistency of toothpaste.

6 Plan the sequence of tile laying so that you don't work yourself into a corner. Scoop thinset mortar onto the floor, and spread it around using the smooth side of a notched trowel. Then use the notched side to comb it. Hold the trowel at a consistent 45-degree angle, barely scraping the floor, to achieve a smooth, even surface. Do not cover the layout lines.

7 Place the first two tiles alongside the layout lines. Give them a slight twist and a push to embed them. Use spacers to keep the tiles the correct distance apart. Also use spacers against a tub or anywhere the edge of the tiles will be visible.

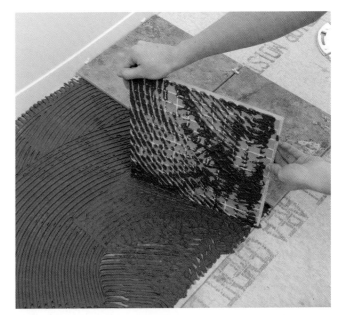

8 Every once in a while, lift a newly set tile to make sure that the thinset is adhering. There should be at least 75-percent coverage. If not, you may need to spread a thin layer of thinset onto the back of each tile using the straight edge of the trowel. If sticking continues to be a problem, the thinset may be starting to dry out. If so, try re-troweling over it. Or scrape it up, and mix a new batch.

Continued on next page

Installing a Ceramic-Tile Floor, cont'd.

9 Continue laying tiles. If four tiles meet at a corner, as shown here, you can set one spacer into each corner. Otherwise, set the spacers upright, two to a side. Every 10 min. or so, stand back; check the layout; and make any needed adjustments.

10 Use a level or a straight board to check that the tiles form an even surface. If a tile is high, it may help to tap it using a board and a hammer. If that doesn't help or if the tile is low, pry it up and remove or add thinset as needed.

13 If you have unglazed natural stone or quarry tiles, carefully paint their surfaces—but not their edges—with acrylic sealer, and allow it to dry; otherwise, grouting will create a haze that is difficult to clean. Mix a batch of fortified grout. Apply it using a grout float. Hold the float nearly flat to push it into the joints. Push in at least two directions at all points.

14 Now tilt the float up, and use it to scrape away most of the excess grout. Move at an angle to the grout lines to avoid digging in. Watch for gaps in the grout, and fill them as you go.

15 Use a large dampened sponge to wipe the surfaces. Press lightly so that you don't dig into the grout joints. Rinse the sponge often. You'll need to go over the surface several times. Watch the grout lines carefully, and use the sponge to achieve lines that are consistent in depth. Allow the surface to dry; then buff it using a dry, clean cloth.

11 After a few rows, press a level or other straightedge against a row to make sure it's straight. Continue to examine the tiles with a critical eye, and adjust tiles as soon as possible; the thinset will not allow you to make adjustments after 15 min. or so. If needed, pry up a tile; scrape off the thinset; and apply new thinset to set it perfectly.

12 Allow the thinset to harden overnight or longer. Use a screwdriver or awl to pry up and remove all of the spacers. Wipe (and if needed, scrape) the surface clean of mortar. If any mortar has squeezed up to within $1/8$ in. of the tile surface, scrape it away using a screwdriver or putty knife; otherwise, it can show through the grout.

Setting Oversize Tiles

If your tiles are 16 inches or larger in either dimension, a trowel with larger notches—either $3/8$ or $1/2$ inch—is recommended **❶**. The thicker thinset bed will help ensure even and complete coverage. Troweling on the thicker mortar is only slightly more difficult than using a smaller-notched trowel **❷**.

Patterned Ceramic or Stone Flooring

For a modest investment in additional materials and a few extra hours of your time, you can install a floor with a border, a central decorative medallion, or scattered accents. Many home centers and tile stores carry accent tiles or mosaic strips made to go with certain field tiles. In some cases you can buy field tiles with corners cut off to accommodate diamond-shaped accents at the junction of four tiles.

For a border, central feature, or any other pattern that must be centered on the floor, measure the room and make a scale drawing showing where each tile will go. (Don't forget to factor in the width of the grout joints.) Plan for a border that is equidistant from the walls on all four sides or a medallion that is centered between at least two—if not all four—walls. A tile salesperson can help you with the planning.

A striking angled checkerboard pattern, above, is made by alternating 12-in. field tiles with 12-in. mosaic sheets.

To create this pattern, right, the field tiles (which are natural marble) were first laid in the center of the floor; then the border tiles were cut to fit and installed around the perimeter.

Setting Diamond Accents

Diamond accents may be scattered here and there on the floor or set in a regular sequence. Getting the saw set up for making precise cuts to accommodate the diamond pieces may take a few tries, so practice on scrap pieces. (Cut the corners off of four tiles; then see whether you get the right grout lines or not after setting them out with the diamond piece before trying on the real thing.)

Set the tiles in a dry run, and hold the accent tile in position. Use a wide carpenter's pencil to mark for the cuts; the line should allow for a grout line the same width as the other lines on the floor ❶. Use a wet-cutting tile saw to cut the corners. For the type of saw shown, you'd set the rip guide and use an angle square to maintain a 45-degree angle ❷. Other saws with moving trays have angle guides that attach to the tray. Sand the cut edge using a hand sander or a random-orbit sander. Sand just enough to ease the sharpness of the edge ❸. Test the pattern before you install it onto troweled thinset. Use spacers for the accent ❹. If the spacers don't fit exactly, visually center the accent tile without spacers.

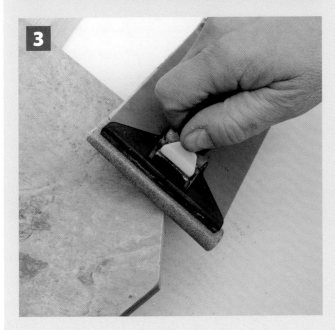

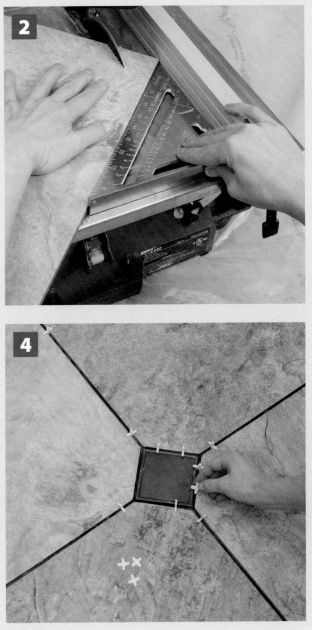

Mosaic Floor Tiles

They say that small tiles make a room look larger, so it's not surprising that many bathrooms have floors made up of hundreds of little mosaic tiles. Fortunately, those tiles come in 12-inch-square sheets, making them easy to lay.

Follow most of the instructions on pages 196-205 for preparing the floor, setting the tiles, and grouting. There are some differences, however:

■ When planning the layout, you cannot hide an out-of-square wall with a wide row of tiles. Because the individual tiles are so small, it will be obvious if a wall is not parallel or is wavy. You may be able to lay the job out so that only one wall—preferably, a wall that is not conspicuous—shows the out-of-square condition. If not, you may be better off installing larger tiles instead.

■ Where 75-percent thinset coverage is fine for large tiles, in a mosaic installation you need 100-percent coverage so that each individual tile is set in mortar. The mortar should be just the right consistency—wet enough for sticking easily but not so wet that it oozes up through the grout joints.

■ Grouting is slightly more difficult because there are so many grout lines. Mix the grout so that it is slightly soupy—more like mayonnaise than toothpaste—and so will easily sink into all the nooks and crannies. And spend plenty of time pressing and scraping, inspecting as you go

This 1930s look, opposite left, is made of mosaic sheets that have weaving patterns around center black squares.

Cutting mosaic sheets into single-tile rows, opposite right, creates a frame for this floor. Field tiles are cut to fit between the rows.

Installing Mosaic Floor Tiles

• Chalk line and other layout tools • Knee pads and protective eyewear • Fortified thinset mortar • Notched trowel of a size recom-float and large sponge • Caulk to match the grout color

1 You can remove a row of tiles or individual tiles simply by slicing through the webbing or (as shown here) the glue attachments. Here we show removing a tile in to install an accent tile.

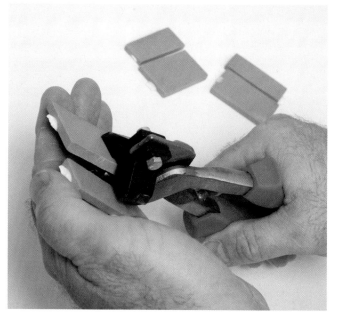

2 You can cut individual tiles with a wet-cutting tile saw or by scoring with a snap cutter and then using tile nippers to complete the cut. (See page 139.) Or use a pair of hand-held tile cutters: score the line with the cutter's wheel; position the tile; and squeeze the handles to complete the cut.

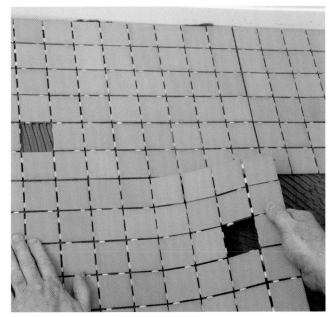

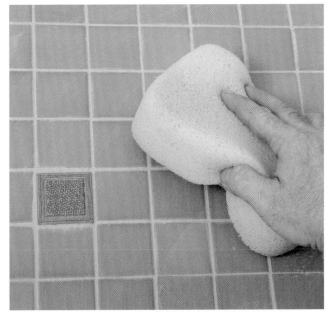

3 Trowel on mortar that is fairly wet and thick enough to embed all of the tiles but not so thick that it will seep up through the joints. Set the sheets carefully, so you don't have to slide them more than ½ in. or so, and press firmly at all points. You may need to back-butter accent tiles with a thin layer of thinset.

4 Apply fairly wet grout with long, sweeping strokes of the float, moving in several directions at all points. Wipe with a damp sponge that you repeatedly rinse, watching the joints carefully and filling in any gaps that appear. Wipe the surface several times; allow it to dry; and buff it using a clean, dry cloth.

Installing Vinyl Sheet Flooring

A vinyl sheet presents a continuous, watertight surface with no joints. That, together with its low price, makes it a popular choice for bathroom floors. Installation can be pretty quick, and you don't have to lay backer board. You must work methodically and carefully, however, because one cutting mistake can ruin the job.

The subfloor does not have to be rock-solid as for ceramic tile, but it must be exceptionally smooth; even small holes and protrusions will show through. If needed, apply sheets of ¼-in. plywood underlayment, using a power stapler. Fill the joints and holes with flooring patch, and sand the surface smooth; the whole floor should feel smooth when you run your hand over it. You can also install vinyl sheet flooring over existing vinyl tile or other flooring, as long as it is smooth and even.

Buy a sheet wide enough so that you won't need to make a seam in the middle of the floor. Some products call for adhesive only around the perimeter, while others require adhesive at all points. Remove the toilet and any other obstructions, as well as the base shoe or base molding. Sweep, vacuum, and damp-wipe the subfloor to remove absolutely all debris, no matter how small.

Installing Vinyl Sheet Flooring

• Straightedge • Utility knife • Chalk line • Floor roller

1 Lay the sheet on a large flat surface. If the sheet came with a paper template, cut it to size; test it on the floor; and use it as a pattern for cutting the sheet. If not, start by cutting the sheet a few inches larger than the room. Use a straightedge and utility knife with a sharp blade.

4 To trim the vinyl along a wall, use a framing square or other thin straightedge to guide a cut that runs close to the wall. (A level does not work.) Leave a ⅛-in. gap between the flooring and the wall.

• 6- or 16-foot wide roll of vinyl sheet flooring • Vinyl flooring adhesive • Small-notched trowel made for vinyl adhesive

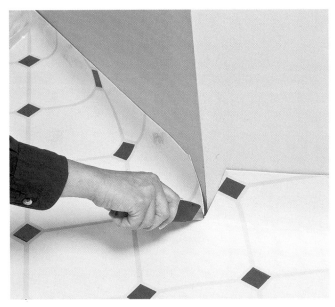

2 With a helper, roll up and carry the sheet into the bathroom, and unroll it, taking care not to crease the sheet. To cut at an outside corner, slit the sheet margin down to the floor; take care not to cut too far, or the cut will be visible.

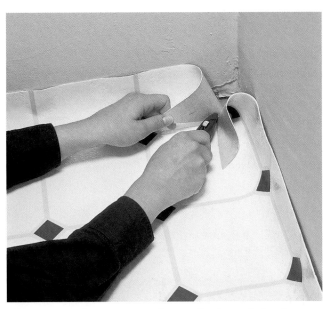

3 At an inside corner, cut diagonally through the sheet margin until the vinyl can lie flat. Press the sheet gently onto the floor at both sides of the cut. Again, take care not to cut too far. Make sure the sheet does not shift position as you work.

5 Once you are sure of the fit, roll one-half of the sheet back to the center of the room. Vacuum and damp-mop away all dust and debris; then spread the adhesive on the bared floor, holding the trowel at a consistent angle so the adhesive is uniformly thick. Roll the flooring back into place. Repeat the procedure for the other half of the floor.

6 Use a rented floor roller to force out any air bubbles. Start in the center of the room, and work out to the edges. Reinstall the toilet and base trim.

8
Wiring and Plumbing Methods

Some of the projects in this book call for a basic understanding of your electrical and plumbing systems, as well as specific techniques for connecting wiring and pipes. In most cases, the short instructions in this chapter will enable you to do the work safely and securely. If you feel lost at any point or would like greater understanding, however, consult the Creative Homeowner books *Ultimate Guide: Wiring* and *Ultimate Guide: Plumbing*. If you are still confused or unsure, don't take chances; call in a professional electrician or plumber.

Safety first! Above all, that means shutting off the power or the water, then testing that the power or water is off before beginning work.

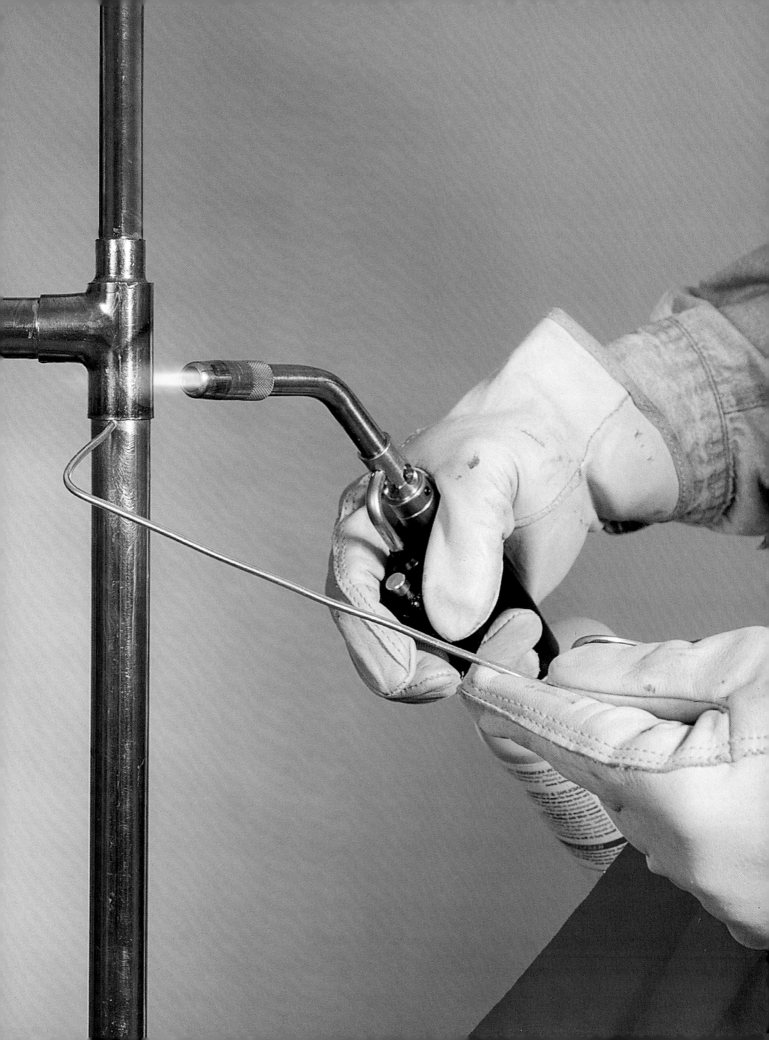

Understanding Bathroom Wiring

If you plan to add new lights, a heater, a vent fan/light combo, radiant heating, or other electrical service, take the time to learn about your bathroom wiring. That means gaining a basic understanding of general household wiring as well.

Working Safely

Safety is consideration number-one when working with wiring. Even a split-second mistake can result in injury or, worse, death. Now that you're sufficiently scared, we should add that by taking careful precautions, you can work safely on your wiring.

Get to know the electrical service-entrance panel. This is where you come to shut off power before working on your wiring. Keep the area clear so that it is easy to get access to, and have a flashlight nearby. There should be a helpful chart telling which circuits operate which rooms and services; if not, take the time to make one. Before working on a circuit, go to the service panel; open its door; and flip off the circuit breaker. Then use a voltage detector to test that power is off. Place a sign on the panel telling family members not to turn the breaker back on until you are finished working.

The Service-Entrance Panel

The main service-entrance panel is the distribution center for household electricity. It is shown on the opposite page with the cover removed (something you need do only when installing a new circuit). Incoming red and black hot wires connect to the main breaker and energize the individual "branch" circuit breakers that are snapped into place. Hot (black, red, or colored) wires connected to the various circuit breakers carry electricity to appliances, fixtures, and receptacles throughout the house. White and bare-copper (or green) wires connect to the neutral and grounding bus bars, respectively.

Keep a well-maintained flashlight near your service panel, and stand on a rubber mat or dry boards (wearing rubber-soled shoes) when working on the panel.

Before working on a circuit, shut off power; then test using a voltage tester to be sure that the power is off. Test both outlets on a receptacle. After removing the cover plate and pulling out the receptacle or switch, test the wires as well.

Loading Circuits

Branch circuit breakers are safety devices that shut off power when the circuit is overloaded—meaning that there is too much electrical demand, which causes wires to overheat dangerously. It's important that no circuit is overloaded. When adding new service or replacing one electrical device with another that uses more power, you should do some calculations to be sure that the new wattage or amperage will not be too much.

Some electricity basics: The force running through all household wires is the same—120 volts. (Bathrooms usually have only 120-volt circuits; 240-volt circuits are used for high-energy users such as large heaters, ovens, cooktops, and the like.) But different fixtures and appliances use different amounts of power. Wattage (or watts) refers to the amount of power an electrical device consumes. Amperes (amps) describes the capacity of the wires. Thicker wire can handle more amps, and thus more watts. Bathroom circuits are almost always either 15-amp, and connected to 14-gauge wire, or 20-amp, supplied by thicker 12-gauge wire.

Fixtures and appliances have labels that give an energy-use rating in terms of either watts or amps. The basic calculation is: amps × volts = watts. A 120-volt, 15-amp circuit has a total capacity of 15 amps, or 1,800 watts; a 120-volt, 20-amp circuit has a total capacity of 20 amps, or 2,400 watts. But electrical codes require that electrical users not exceed "safe capacity," which is 80 percent of total capacity. That means a 15-amp circuit should supply no more than 12 amps, or 1,440 watts, and a 20-amp circuit should supply no more than 16 amps, or 1,920 watts.

To calculate whether a circuit will be overloaded or not, add up all of the electrical users—including appliances plugged into receptacles—in terms of watts or amps. For instance, if a 20-amp circuit supplies light fixtures that

Service-Entrance Panel

Also called the circuit-breaker panel, the main service-entrance panel (SEP) is the distribution center for the electricity you use in your home. Incoming red and black hot wires connect to the main breaker and energize the other circuit breakers that are snapped into place. Hot (black or red) wires connected to the various circuit breakers carry electricity to appliances, fixtures, and receptacles throughout the house. White and bare-copper wires connect to the neutral and grounding bus bars, respectively. (Representative 120-volt and 120/240-volt circuits are shown.)

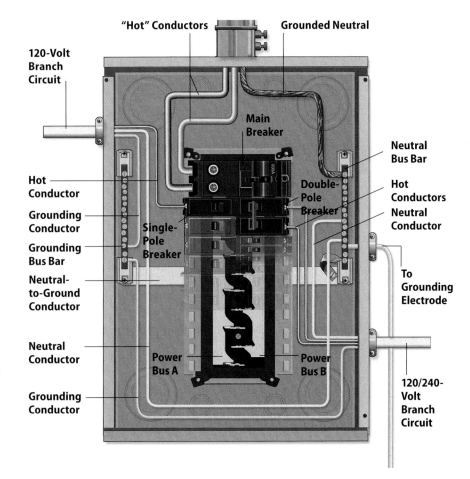

use a total of four 100-watt bulbs (400 watts), plus a vent fan rated at 2 amps (2 × 120 = 240 watts), and it supplies a receptacle that often services a hair dryer rated at 1,800 watts, then using the hair dryer with all of the lights and the fan on will pull 2,440 watts—which will overload the circuit. (You may want to find a more energy-efficient hair dryer.)

If you want to install a wall heater or other high-use appliance, run the numbers to see whether you can piggyback on an existing circuit or not. If not, you'll need to install a new circuit. (See pages 218-19.)

Making the Connections

Once the power is safely off and you are certain that you will not overload a circuit, it's time to connect the wiring. All electrical connections must be made inside an electrical box that is approved by local building and electrical codes. (Many municipalities allow plastic boxes, while some require that metal boxes be used.)

Stripping Wires

The goal of stripping is to remove ½ to ¾ inch of insulation without damaging the wire itself. Don't try to do this using a knife, though you may be tempted; you run the risk of nicking the bare wire, which can cause the connection to fail. Use a wire stripper.

Connecting to a Terminal

When attaching wires to the terminals of a switch or receptacle, connect to the terminal screws rather than the push-in holes, which are not as reliable. (Some high-end devices have push-in holes with setscrews that clamp the wire firmly; they work very well.) Connect black or colored wires to brass terminals, white neutral wires to silver terminals, and the grounding wire to the grounding screw, which is usually green.

To make a firm connection, strip the wire; then wrap it clockwise most of the way around the screw shank. Tighten the screw firmly.

Splicing Wires

To splice solid wires together, strip ¾ to 1 inch of insulation from each; then grab the two wire ends with a pair of lineman's pliers; twist them together in a clockwise direction; and screw on a wire connector. Some people prefer to skip the twisting part: they just hold the wires next to each other and twist on the wire connector to make the connection. Either way, tug on the wires to make sure the connection is firm. To splice a stranded fixture lead to a solid house wire, spirally twist the stranded wire around the solid wire, and cap the splice with a wire connector. To join two stranded wires, twist them together with your fingers; then add a wire connector.

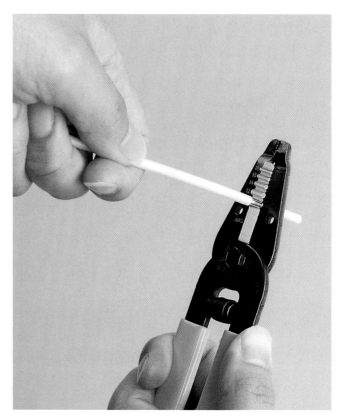

To use a manual wire stripper, insert the wire into the matching-gauge hole; close the stripper to cut through the insulation; and pull the insulation off.

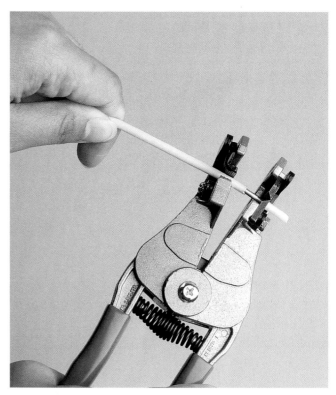

An automatic wire stripper cuts and strips in one step: just insert the wire, and squeeze the handles.

Working with Cable

If you will run new cable, most local building departments allow NM (nonmetallic) cable, but some require metal-clad cable. "Two-wire" NM cable has two insulated wires—a black-clad hot wire and a white-clad neutral—plus a bare grounding wire. Three-wire cable has the addition of a red-clad wire.

Use a cable ripper to slice the center of the sheathing on NM cable without damaging the wire insulation ❶. Pull back 8 to 10 inches of the sheathing; then use diagonal-cutting pliers to cut away the excess sheathing and paper wrapping ❷. Connect cable firmly to an approved electrical box. You may need to use a cable clamp, or the box may have its own clamp.

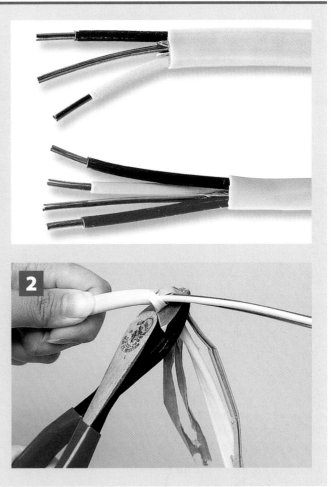

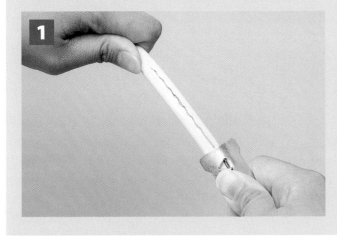

Cut-In (Remodel) Boxes

Many different sizes and types of metal and plastic electrical boxes are available for various uses. Be sure to use boxes that are approved for use in your area. When working in a space with finished walls, it's usually easiest to use a cut-in box, also called an old-work or remodel box. Here we show a round fixture box, but rectangular switch boxes are also available. Trace a template of the box on the wall or ceiling, and cut through the drywall ❶. Run cable into the box, and clamp it. Insert the box in the opening, and adjust the side wings ❷. Tighten the mounting screws to bring the wings firmly against the back of the drywall ❸ (viewed from inside the wall).

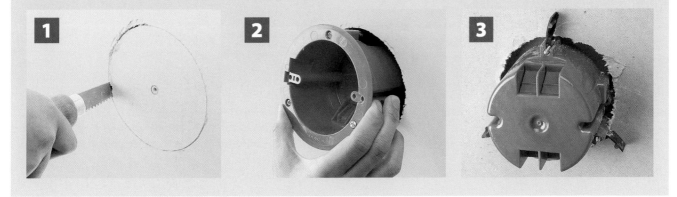

Adding a New Circuit

If you have determined that you need a new electrical circuit, plan the path for the cable. Use 14-gauge wire for a 15-amp circuit or 12-gauge wire for a 20-amp circuit. The cable must be hidden inside walls or run along exposed joists or studs in basements or other unfinished spaces.

Adding a New Circuit

• Flashlight • Screwdriver and hammer • Drill-driver • Cable that meets local electrical codes • Cable staples • Side-cutting pliers

1 Open the service-entrance-panel door, and turn off the main circuit breaker. Remove the screws that hold the cover in place, and pull off the cover.

2 The locations of the current circuits should be labeled on the cover door. Run cable from the panel to the bathroom, leaving plenty of extra cable at both ends.

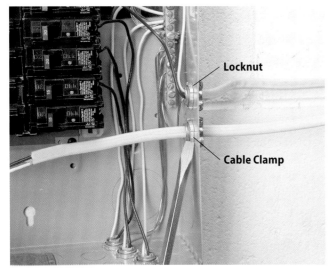

Locknut

Cable Clamp

5 Finger-tighten the cable clamp against the side of the panel. Then use a screwdriver and hammer to drive the locknut clockwise until it is tight.

Hot Bus

Neutral Bus

Grounding Bus

6 Run all of the wires around the perimeter of the panel, keeping an orderly arrangement. Run the black and/ or colored wire(s) to the location of the new breaker and the white and grounding wires to open holes in the neutral and grounding bus bars, respectively.

You may be able to run cable down through a baseplate and into the basement. Or you may need to remove sections of drywall to run the cable. Staple the cable to the centers of studs or joists, where drywall nails or screws cannot reach it.

Connect the cable to the fixture or device in the bathroom using appropriate clamps or connectors. Because you will need to shut off power to the entire house, do the work during the day; if there is insufficient light or it's nighttime, have a helper hold a flashlight while you work.

• Circuit breaker of the required amperage and of the same make as the panel • Wire and cable strippers • Cable clamp

---

3 Look for an open slot in the panel where you can install the new circuit breaker. If a breaker has no wire attached to it, you may be able to simply run the wire to that breaker.

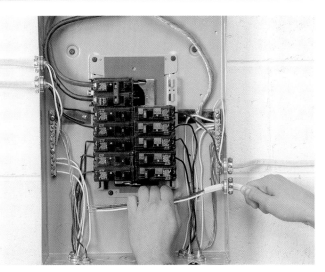

4 Strip as much as 2 ft. of sheathing, so the wires can travel around the panel if needed. Pry out a knockout plate; install a cable clamp; and push the cable through, up to the cable sheathing.

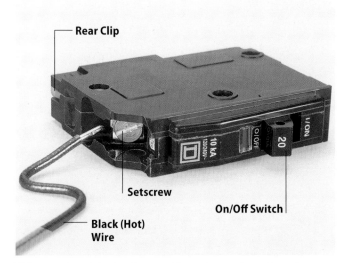

7 Cut the white and grounding wires to length; strip about ¾ in. of the insulation; poke them into their respective holes; and tighten the setscrews. Run the black and/or colored wire(s) to the new breaker; poke it into the hole; and tighten the setscrew. Push the breaker into its slot so that it seats firmly onto the bus bars, like the other breakers. It should snap into place.

8 Remove the knockout plate (on the face of the cover) that falls where the new breaker is located. Reinstall the cover. Label the circuit on the inside of the door, and turn on the main breaker.

Understanding Bathroom Plumbing

Bathroom plumbing accomplishes three basic tasks:

- Deliver hot and cold water to fixtures and appliances
- Carry waste to the sewer or septic system
- Vent the waste drainpipes to the outside so that wastewater can flow freely

Your house may have intermediate valves that shut off water to a part of the house, like the bathroom or kitchen. Near most fixtures you will find stop valves, also called fixture shutoff valves (right), usually where the supply pipes emerge from the wall or floor. If any sink or toilet does not have a stop valve, it's a good idea to hire a plumber to install one.

The Supply System

Every water-using fixture except the toilet requires separate hot- and cold-water supply pipes. Stop valves for each, also called fixture shutoff valves, should be located near each fixture, so you can shut off water to that fixture separately.

Supply pipes in an older home may be made of galvanized steel with threaded connectors. These pipes tend to collect mineral deposits and rust over time, which causes them to clog and perhaps leak. Homes built after World War II are likely to have copper supply pipes. Some homes built recently have supply pipes made of CPVC (chlorinated polyvinyl chloride), a solid plastic, or PEX (cross-linked polyethylene), a flexible material. Main supply pipes are typically ¾ inch in (inside) diameter; ½-inch pipes run to individual fixtures.

Shut off the Water

Before you remove a fixture or start to work on the plumbing system, you must shut off the water to that part of the system (shutoff valve near right) and test to verify that water is off. The main shutoff valve is often located where the home's water supply pipe enters the house or (in many municipal water-supply systems) in a "Buffalo box" located underground in the front or rear of the house. The valve may look like that shown far right, or it may have a round handle that you have to rotate a number of turns to shut off.

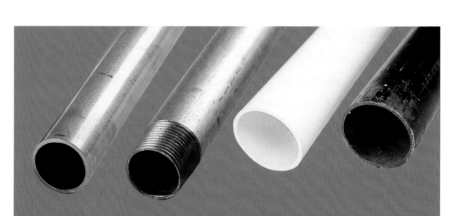

Pipe Types

The most common pipe materials (left to right) are:

- **Copper, used mostly for hot- and cold-water supply pipes and sometimes for DWV pipes.**
- **Galvanized steel, for supply pipes and sometimes for drainpipes in older homes.**
- **PVC, the most common material for DWV pipes in newer homes.**
- **Cast iron, for DWV pipes in older homes.**
- **CPVC, for supply pipes (not shown).**
- **PEX, for supply pipes (not shown).**
- **ABS (acrylonitrile butadiene styrene), a black material sometimes used for DWV pipes in newer homes (not shown).**

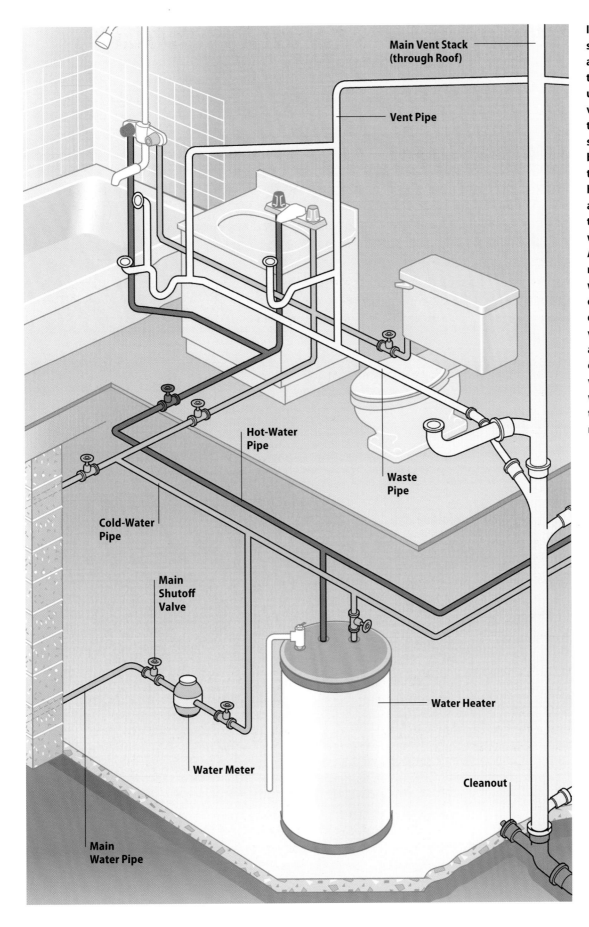

Main Vent Stack
(through Roof)

Vent Pipe

Hot-Water
Pipe

Waste
Pipe

Cold-Water
Pipe

Main
Shutoff
Valve

Water Heater

Water Meter

Cleanout

Main
Water Pipe

In this typical system, water arrives from the municipal utility or a private well. All of the cold-water supply lines branch from this main line; hot-water lines are first routed through the water heater. All fixtures receiving water are also connected to drainpipes and vent pipes, and converge on a soil, or vent, stack, which extends through the roof.

The DWV System

The pipes that carry waste to the sewer and vent fixtures to the outside work together as a drain-waste-vent (DWV) system. Waste pipes drain water, while vent pipes allow outside air into the system. (Without this air, pipes may gurgle or even stop up; vent pipes also remove odorous and noxious gases.) The soil stack is a vertical large-diameter pipe that carries waste down to the sewer and vents air through the roof. DWV lines may be anywhere from 1½ to 4 inches in diameter, depending on their purpose. National and local plumbing codes have strict (and often complicated) requirements for pipe size.

Older homes may have pipes made of cast iron, which is very difficult to work with. Newer homes have plastic (black ABS, or more commonly, white PVC) DWV pipes, which are easy to cut and assemble.

Drainpipes. Waste lines must slope at code-approved angles to carry water to the sewer. Small-diameter pipes run from sinks, showers, and tubs to feed into the soil stack, which usually sits in the wall behind the toilet. Each fixture requires a trap, a curved part near the fixture drain to trap water, preventing sewer gas from entering the room. Toilets have built-in traps.

Vent pipes. When planning a new fixture (rather than a replacement), the first consideration is usually the vent-pipe system, which must comply with often-complicated plumbing codes. In a simple arrangement with a sink, toilet, and tub on the same wall, the soil stack is simply extended through the roof to provide a vent. When plumbing fixtures are on more than one wall, set apart from each other, or more than a few feet away from the stack, more vents may be required.

Drainpipes and Fittings

Drainage pipes are assembled with a variety of fittings. Here are some of the most common: (A) cleanout plug, (B) threaded adapter; (C) coupling (D) cross, (E) ground-joint adapter, (F) street 90-degree elbow, (G) 3 x 1½-inch T-fitting, (H) 45-degree elbow, (I) 3 x 2-inch Y-fitting, (J) sanitary T-fitting, (K) coupling, (L) trap arm, (M) fixture trap.

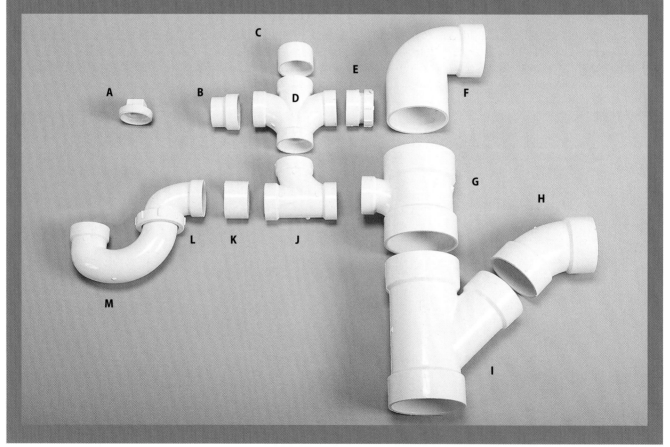

Cutting and Joining Pipes

Most modern pipes are relatively easy to cut and join. Be sure to comply with local codes in order to assemble them correctly.

Plastic Pipe

Here we show assembling small-diameter supply tubing; use the same methods for larger drainpipes.

Cutting and Joining Plastic Pipe

• CPVC tubing and fittings • Miter box and backsaw (or other cutter) • Utility knife • CPVC primer and cement • Marker

1 Cut the tube using a miter box and backsaw, power miter saw, hacksaw, or special plastic pipe saw. After cutting, scrape the end with a utility knife to remove any burrs resulting from the cut.

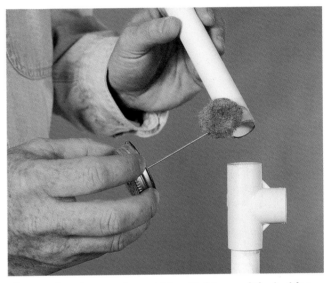

2 Apply primer to the outside of tubing and the insides of fittings. Do not skip this step, or the joint may leak.

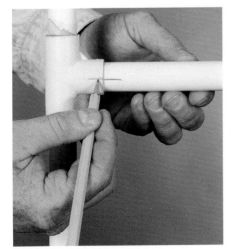

3 Dry-assemble all the components, and test to make sure they will fit. Make alignment marks to ensure that you will install them in the correct configuration.

4 Take apart the assembly, keeping track of where each part goes. To make a connection, apply pipe cement to the inside of the fitting and the outside of the tubing end.

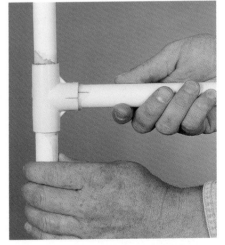

5 Immediately push the tube firmly into the fitting; then twist ½ in. or so, and hold the assembly still for a count of 10. Move on to the next section, but wait an hour or so before using the tubing.

Cutting and Joining Copper Tubing

• Copper tubing and fittings • Tubing cutter • Combination tool • Flux, brush, solder, and torch

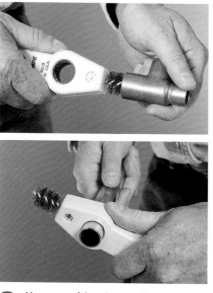

1 To cut copper tubing, twist to open the jaws of a tubing cutter; insert the tube into the cutter; and tighten the jaws until they start to bite. Rotate the cutter one full turn; tighten a bit more; rotate the cutter again; and repeat until you have cut the tube. Test-fit several pieces to be sure that they will fit.

2 Use a combination tool or strips of plumber's sandpaper to clean the inside of the fittings and the outside of the tubing ends. Scrape until the copper is shiny, and don't touch the cleaned portion while you work.

3 Spread flux on the inside of the fittings and around the outside of the tubing using the small brush that comes with the flux. Keep the brush and the can of flux protected from dust and debris, so you can apply it cleanly. Assemble the tubing and fittings.

4 Pull 12 in. or so of solder out from the roll, and bend it into an L-shape. Turn on the torch, and adjust the flame so that the tip is blue colored. Direct the blue tip to both sides of the fitting (not the tube). When the fitting is hot enough, touch the solder to the joint; it will suck into the joint.

5 The joint is successfully soldered when it stops drawing solder and new solder starts to spill out. When this happens, immediately wipe away any excess with a rag. With practice, you can solder all three joints of a T-fitting quickly.

Protect the Area   *TIP*

When soldering close to combustible material, use a piece of flashing or an old cookie sheet to protect these areas. You may need to hold the flashing in place with duct tape.

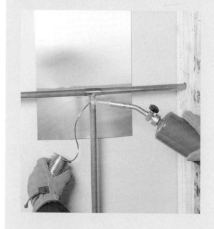

The PEX Option

In many areas of the country, PEX (cross-linked polyethylene) has been approved for water supply lines. The tubing is inexpensive and easy to assemble, and it snakes easily around corners. Buy PEX tubing, fittings, and a crimping tool that match; different types use different tools.

Cut PEX using a plastic tubing cutter, which simply slices cleanly through to make a cut that is burr free ❶. Install the appropriate conversion fitting to make the transition from galvanized (shown here), copper, or plastic supply tubing ❷. Barbed PEX fittings, like this coupling, are available in plastic and brass. Slip on a crimp ring, and slide the tube onto the fitting. Use a special tool to tighten the crimp ring and make a water-tight connection ❸. Here the connection is made to a stop valve. A variety of fittings and valves with barbed ends are available ❹. Here is a reducing T-fitting, which connects two ½-in. tubes to a ¾-in. tube ❺.

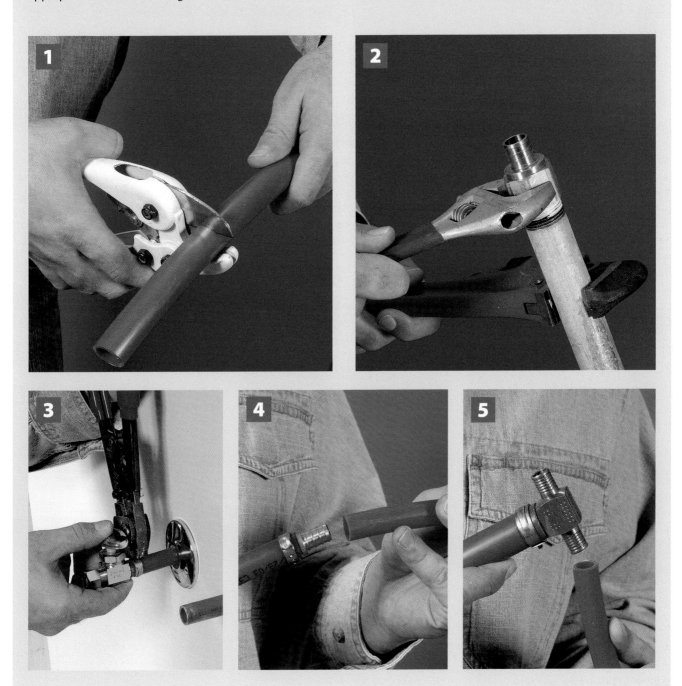

Glossary

Ampere (amp): The standard unit of electrical current. See also *volt* and *watt*.

Anti-scald valve: A fitting in a tub/shower valve that automatically responds to changes in line water pressure to prevent sudden spikes in temperature.

Backsplash: Either (A) a short (usually about 4-in.) strip of wood or tile that rests on top of the countertop at the wall, or (B) the wall area between a countertop and the bottom of wall cabinets.

Baseboard: A trim board attached to the bottom of a wall where it meets the floor.

Base shoe: A narrow trim piece often attached to the bottom of a baseboard.

Bidet: A toilet-shaped bathroom fixture that supplies water for personal hygiene.

Cable: Two or more wires encased in protective plastic or metal sheathing.

Cement backer board: A rigid panel made primarily of cementitious material reinforced by a fiber mat that is used as a substrate for tiles in wet areas. These sheets will not rot even when they are soaked with water for prolonged periods. (Also *fiber-cement backer board; concrete backer board*)

Code: Locally or nationally enforced mandates that regulate structural design, materials, plumbing, and electrical systems.

Countertop: The work surface of a counter, often 36 inches above the floor. It may be made of plastic laminate, granite or other stone, or composite stone material.

Dry run: The process of temporarily arranging tiles or other elements to check the layout before applying adhesive.

Duct: A passageway made of sheet-metal or plastic-and-wire tubing that carries air from a vent fan to the outside.

DWV (drain-waste-vent): In plumbing, the system of pipes and fittings that carries away wastewater.

Escutcheon: A decorative plate that covers a hole in the wall around pipes.

Fiber-cement backer board: See *cement backer board*.

Fixture: Any fixed part of the structural design, such as a tub, toilet, or sink.

Fixture shutoff valve: See *stop valve*.

Flux: Paste-like material applied to the surface of copper pipes and fittings prior to soldering (sweating); an essential part of the bonding process.

Full bath: A bathroom that contains a tub and/or shower, plus a sink and toilet.

Ground: The connection between electrical circuits and equipment and the earth. This may be achieved by a separate grounding wire or by metal sheathing or conduit.

GFCI (ground-fault circuit interrupter): An electrical receptacle (outlet) or circuit breaker that shuts down when it senses even a tiny discrepancy in electrical current to prevent electrical shock. GFCIs are required by code in areas subject to dampness, such as bathrooms.

Grout: A binder and filler applied to the joints between ceramic or stone tile.

Grout float: A flat, rubber-faced trowel-like tool used to apply grout.

Half-bath: A bathroom that contains only a toilet and a sink. (Also powder room.)

Inlet: Threaded tube under a faucet or toilet tank onto which the flexible supply tube is screwed.

Lavatory (Lav): a fixed bowl or basin with running water and drainpipe that is used for washing. (Also sink.)

Mastic (organic mastic): A ready-mix adhesive used for applying tiles to a wall; sometimes also used for floor tiles.

Notched trowel: See *trowel.*

Organic mastic: See *mastic.*

Overflow: A plumbing outlet positioned on a tub or sink that allows water to escape if a faucet is left open and the tub or sink fills up to a certain level.

P-trap: A curved part of a fixture drain, usually shaped like a sideways "P," that fills with water to create a seal to prevent gases from coming into a house's interior. (Also *trap.*)

Pedestal sink: A stand-alone lavatory with a supporting column.

Pop-up assembly: A mechanism that allows you to move a sink or tub's stopper up or down to allow water to drain or fill the bowl. Some newer fixtures do not have a pop-up drain, and instead have a stopper that you control with your fingers or toes.

Powder room: See *half-bath.*

Resilient flooring: Floor covering made of flexible material such as vinyl, rubber, cork, or linoleum. Wood flooring is sometimes also considered resilient.

Roughing in: The installation of the water-supply and DWV pipes before the fixtures are put in place.

Sconce: A light fixture that is mounted on a wall.

Shutoff valve: A device set into a water line to allow for interruption of the flow of water.

Sink: See *lavatory.*

Soil stack: The main vertical drainpipe in a house that carries waste to the sewer line and extends through the roof to vent the system. (Also vent stack.)

Stop valve (fixture shutoff valve): A shutoff valve that controls water supplying a single fixture. It is usually accessible from inside a room, and there is one for hot water and one for cold water. See also *shutoff valve.*

Studs: Vertical members of a framed wall, usually 2x4s or 2x6s installed every 16 inches.

Subfloor: The supporting surface below a finished floor. In newer homes, the subfloor is usually made of plywood; in older homes it is usually made of planks.

Supply tube: A flexible tube, often covered with braided metal, that makes the connection between the stop valve and a faucet's or toilet's inlet. Supply tubes are not allowed inside walls—only where they are visible and easily reached.

Taping knife: A flat-bladed tool with a handle that comes in various widths and is used to apply joint compound or spackle to a wall.

Thinset: A cement-based mortar adhesive applied to a floor or wall for setting tile.

Tongue-and-groove: Boards milled with a protruding tongue on one edge and a slot on the other, so they fit snugly and firmly together when installed side by side.

Trap: See *P-trap.*

Trowel: A flat tool, like a small metal sheet, with a handle used for applying mortar and other adhesives. A notched trowel has teeth that produce a series of evenly spaced ridges.

Vanity: A cabinet that supports a lavatory. It sometimes also includes a countertop.

Vent stack: See *soil stack.*

Volt: A unit of electromotive force. Volts x amps = watts. See also *ampere* and *watt.*

Watt: a measurement of electrical power required or consumed by a fixture or appliance. See also *ampere* and *volt.*

Wire connector: A small plastic cap with a threaded female portion inside, used to connect two or more wires together and to protect them from contact with metal surfaces.

Index

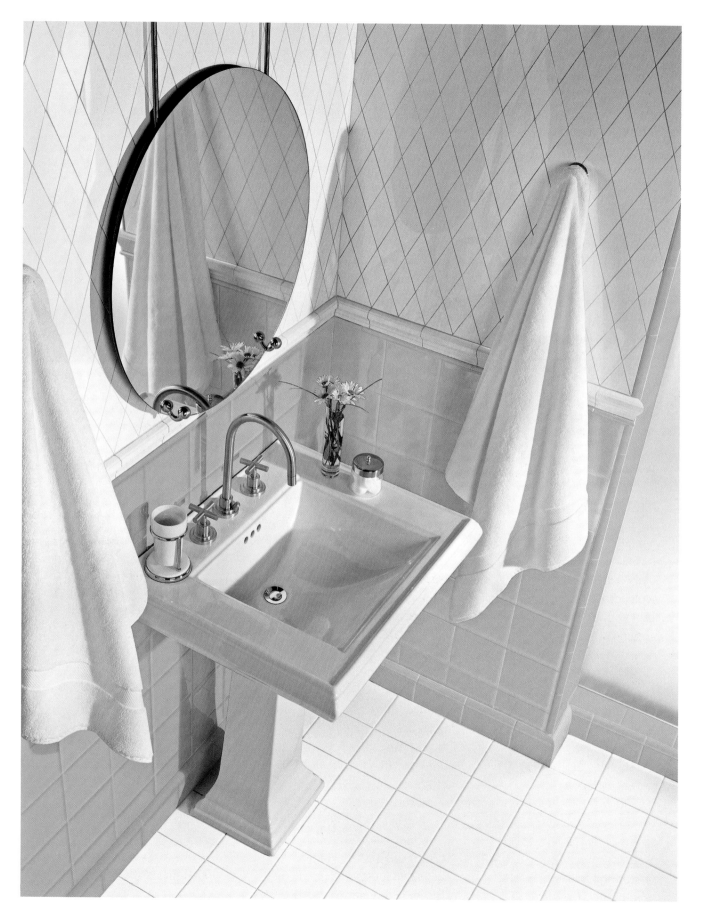

Resource Guide

The following list of manufacturers and associations is meant to be a general guide to additional industry and product-related sources. It is not intended as a listing of products and manufacturers represented by the photographs in this book.

American Bath Factory
www.americanbathfactory.com
(800)454-2284
Corona, CA
Bathtubs, showers, faucets, accessories, vessel sinks

American Olean
www.americanolean.com
(888)268-8453
Dallas, TX
Ceramic tile for floors, walls, and countertops; design tools on the company's Web site

American Standard
www.americanstandard.com
(800)442-1902
Piscataway, NJ
Bathroom faucets and accessories, bathroom furniture, sinks, and vanity tops, toilets and seats, bidets, showers, bathtubs, whirlpools, repair parts

Armstrong
www.armstrong.com
(717)397-0611
Lancaster, PA
Hardwood, laminate, and vinyl flooring, cabinets, and ceilings

Behr Process Corporation (a Masco company)
www.behr.com
(877)237-6158
Santa Ana, CA
Interior and exterior paint products in an extensive range of colors

Dal-Tile Corporation
www.daltile.com
(214)398-1411
Dallas, TX
A variety of tiles for floors, walls, and counters, including porcelain, quarry, terrazzo, ceramic, mosaic, recycled tiles, as well as glass and metal accent tiles

Delta Faucet Company
www.deltafaucetcompany.com
(800)345-3358
Indianapolis, IN
Bathroom faucets for sinks, showers, and bathtubs; bidet fixtures; bath accessories

DuPont
www.dupont.com
(800)906-7765
Wilmington, DE
Corian solid-surface and Zodiaq quartz-surface countertops

The Dutch Boy Group
www.dutchboy.com
(888)521-0199 Cleveland, OH
Interior and exterior paint products, including primers, ceiling paints, porch and floor paint, and faux finishes

Ginger
www.gingerco.com
(949)417-5207
Santa Ana, CA
Bathroom sink, tub, and shower faucets, and bathroom accessories, including lights, shelves, towel bars and hooks, mirrors, and cabinet hardware

Hakatai Enterprises
www.hakatai.com
(888)667-2429
Ashland, OR
Importer and distributor of glass mosaic tile

iapsales.com LLC
www.heateroutlet.com
(800)416-1298
Exeter, NH
A variety of heaters, including electric, gas, water, and radiant heaters and thermostats

Ikea
www.ikea.com
(800)434-4532
Conshohocken, PA
Sinks, faucets, vanities, mirrors, linens, and innovative storage products

Kohler
www.kohler.com
(800)456-4537
Kohler, WI
Sinks, faucets, vanities, bathtubs, toilets, as well as bathroom accessories and storage products

Kraftmaid
www.kraftmaid.com
(888)562-7744
Ann Arbor, MI
Semi-custom cabinetry with a wide selection of door styles and finishes

LBL Lighting
www.lbllighting.com
(800)323-3226
Skokie, IL
A variety of lighting products

Liberty Hardware Manufacturing Corporation (a Delta company)
www.libertyhardware.com
(800)542-3789
Winston-Salem, NC
A variety of hardware products for bathrooms, including bath safety products

Merillat
www.merillat.com
(866)850-8557
Adrian, Michigan
Cabinetry for bath and kitchen, including storage solutions

Moen
www.moen.com
(800)289-6636
North Olmsted, OH
Bathtub, sink, and shower faucets, and bathroom accessories, including hardware, shelves, lighting, and mirrors

Mr. Steam
www.mrsteam.com
(718)937-4500
Long Island City, NY
Steam products, including towel warmers, shower speakers, shower seats, and patented steam systems

Porcher
www.porcher-us.com
(800)359-3261
Piscataway, NJ
Bathroom faucets and accessories, furniture, sinks, toilets and seats, bidets, showers, bathtubs, whirlpools

Robern
www.robern.com
(800)877-2376
Bristol, PA
Cabinets, lighting, mirrors, vanities, and bathroom accessories, including medicine cabinets, mirrors, and vanity storage products

Smith + Noble
smithnoble.com
(888)214-2134
Corona, CA
Window treatments, including shutters, blinds, shades, curtains, draperies, and hardware

Swan Corporation
www.swanstone.com
(800)325-7008
St. Louis, MO
High-performance solid surfaces

Tech Lighting
www.techlighting.com
(800)522.5315
Skokie, IL
Low-voltage lighting systems and light fixtures, including globes made from blown glass

Velux America, Inc.
www.veluxusa.com
(800)888-3589
Greenwood, SC
Skylights, solar tubes, solar water heaters, and blinds

Villeroy & Boch
www.villeroy-boch.com/en/us/
(609)578-4300
Monroe Township, NJ Fixtures, fittings, and furniture

Walker Zanger
www.walkerzanger.com
(818)252-4000
Sylmar, CA
Tiles of all kinds, including mosaic, decorative stone, rustic stone, glass, metal, terra cotta, ceramic, and porcelain

Credits

All photographs by Steve Cory and Diane Slavik unless otherwise noted

Front cover: *top left*, courtesy of Dal-Tile; *top right*, courtesy of Moen; *bottom left*, courtesy of American Standard; *bottom center*, courtesy of Dal-Tile; *bottom right*, courtesy of Kohler **Back cover:** *top right*, courtesy of Moen; *center left*, courtesy of Dal-Tile **Page 1:** courtesy of Moen **Page 2:** courtesy of Kohler **Page 6:** courtesy of Dal-Tile **Pages 8–9:** *all*, courtesy of Moen **Pages 10–11:** courtesy of Moen **Page 12:** *left*, courtesy of Kohler; *right*, courtesy of Moen **Page 13:** courtesy of Dal-Tile **Page 14:** *top*, courtesy of Dal-Tile; *bottom*, courtesy of American Standard **Page 15:** *top*, courtesy of American Standard; *bottom*, courtesy of Dal-Tile **Page 16:** *top*, courtesy of Kohler; *bottom left*, courtesy of Kohler; *bottom right*, courtesy of Kohler **Page 17:** *all*, courtesy of Kohler **Page 18:** *top and bottom left,* courtesy of Kohler; *bottom right*, courtesy of Dal-Tile **Page 19:** courtesy of Moen **Page 20:** *top and bottom left*, courtesy of Kohler; *bottom right*, courtesy of the Dutch Boy Group **Page 21:** *top*, courtesy of Moen; *bottom right*, courtesy of Ikea **Page 22:** *top*, courtesy of Dal-Tile; *bottom*, courtesy of the Dutch Boy Group **Page 23:** *top left and right*, courtesy of Dal-Tile; *bottom*, courtesy of Kohler Page 24 top: courtesy of American Standard **Page 24:** *bottom*, courtesy of Kohler; *bottom right*, courtesy of Tech Lighting **Page 25:** *top left and right*, courtesy of Dal-Tile; *bottom*, courtesy of Kohler **Page 26**: *top*, courtesy of Dal-Tile; *bottom*, courtesy of American Standard **Page 27:** *top*, courtesy of Moen; *center left, center*

right, and bottom right, courtesy of Kohler **Page 28:** top: courtesy of Moen; *bottom*, Dreamstime **Page 29:** *top left and bottom left and right*, courtesy of Kohler; top right, courtesy of Moen **Page 30:** *top and bottom right*, courtesy of the Dutch Boy Group; *bottom left*, courtesy of Moen **Page 31:** *top left*, courtesy of Kohler; *top right*, courtesy of Ikea; *bottom*, courtesy of American Standard **Page 32:** *left*, courtesy of Kohler; *top right*, courtesy of Dal-Tile; *bottom right*, courtesy of Moen **Page 33:** *top*, courtesy of Kohler; *bottom left*, courtesy of American Standard; *bottom right*, courtesy of Dal-Tile **Pages 34–35:** courtesy of Moen **Page 36:** courtesy of Dal-Tile **Page 37:** *top left and right*, courtesy of American Standard; *bottom right*, courtesy of Dal-Tile **Page 38:** *top*, courtesy of Kohler; *bottom*, courtesy of Ikea **Page 39:** courtesy of Dal-Tile **Page 40:** courtesy of Dal-Tile **Page 41:** *top*, courtesy of Walker Zanger; *bottom left and right*, courtesy of Dal-Tile **Page 42:** *top left*, courtesy of American Standard; *top right and bottom two*, John Parsekian/CH **Page 43:** *all*, Freeze Frame/CH **Page 44:** courtesy of American Standard **Page 46:** courtesy of Kohler **Pages 48–49:** *all*, Dave Toht and Rebecca Anderson **Page 50:** courtesy of Kohler **Page 52:** *all*, Merle Henkenius/CH **Page 53:** *all*, Freeze Frame/CH **Page 54:** courtesy of American Standard **Page 55:** *bottom left*, courtesy of Ikea **Pages 58–63:** *all*, Dave Toht and Rebecca Anderson **Page 64:** courtesy of Porcher **Page 66:** courtesy of Dal-Tile **Page 68:** courtesy of Kohler **Page 71:** *all*, Neal Barrett/CH **Page 74:** courtesy of Kohler **Page 75:** *all*, Merle Henkenius/CH **Page 78:** *top*, courtesy of Porcher;

bottom left, courtesy of American Standard **Page 80:** *top*, courtesy of Moen; *bottom middle and right*, Merle Henkenius/CH **Page 81:** *top*, Merle Henkenius/CH; *bottom*, courtesy of American Standard **Pages 82–83:** courtesy of Ginger **Page 84:** *top*, courtesy of Kraftmaid; *bottom*, courtesy of Kohler **Page 85:** *top and bottom right*, courtesy of Kohler; *bottom left*, courtesy of Robern **Page 86:** *left*, courtesy of Robern; *top and bottom right*, Freeze Frame/CH **Page 87:** *all*, Freeze Frame/CH **Page 88:** *left*, courtesy of Ikea; *top and bottom right*, Freeze Frame/CH **Page 89:** *all*, **Freeze Frame/CH Page 90:** *top and bottom left*, courtesy of Liberty Hardware; *bottom right*, courtesy of Ikea **Page 91:** *bottom left*, courtesy of Ikea; *bottom right*, courtesy of Liberty Hardware **Page 98:** courtesy of Ikea **Page 99:** *top*, courtesy of Ginger; *bottom left*: courtesy of Ikea; *bottom right*, courtesy of Moen **Pages 100–101:** *all*, Dave Toht and Rebecca Anderson **Page 102:** *top left*, courtesy of Liberty Hardware; *top right*, courtesy of Liberty Hardware; *bottom three*, Dave Toht and Rebecca Anderson **Page 103:** *all*, Dave Toht and Rebecca Anderson **Page 104:** *top*, courtesy of Merillat; *bottom left and right*: courtesy of Kraftmaid **Page 105:** *top*, courtesy of Kraftmaid; *bottom*, courtesy of Rev-a-Shelf **Pages 106–07:** *all*, courtesy of Kohler **Page 108:** courtesy of American Bath Factory **Page 110:** courtesy of Moen **Page 113:** *top*, courtesy of American Standard **Page 116:** *top*, Freeze Frame/CH; *bottom four*, **Merle Henkenius/CH Pages 118–19:** *all*, courtesy of Swan Corporation **Page 120:** courtesy of American Standard **Page 122:** *left*, courtesy of American

Standard; *top and bottom right*, Freeze Frame/CH **Page 123:** *all*, **Freeze Frame/CH Page 124:** *left and top right*, courtesy of American Bath Factory; *bottom right*, courtesy of Dal-Tile **Page 125:** courtesy of Dal-Tile **Pages 126–27:** *all*, Freeze Frame/CH **Page 128:** *top middle and right*, Freeze Frame/CH; *bottom three*, Merle Henkenius/CH **Page 129:** *all*, Merle Henkenius/CH **Page 130:** *left*, courtesy of Kohler; *top and bottom right*, Merle Henkenius/CH **Page 131:** *all*, Merle Henkenius/CH **Page 132:** courtesy of Dal-Tile **Page 135:** *top left and inset*, Freeze Frame/CH **Page 136:** *left*, courtesy of Ginger **Page 142:** *left*, courtesy of Dal-Tile; *four process photos*, Merle Henkenius/CH **Page 143:** *all*, Merle Henkenius/CH **Page 144:** courtesy of Moen **Pages 146–47:** courtesy of Dal-Tile **Pages 148–49:** *all*, Freeze Frame/CH **Page 150:** *left*, courtesy of Behr Process Corp.; *top and bottom right*, John Parsekian/CH **Page 151:** *all*, John Parsekian **Pages 152–54:** *all*, Dave Toht and Rebecca Anderson **Page 155:** *top two and bottom left*, Dave Toht and Rebecca Anderson; *bottom right*, courtesy of Walker Zanger **Page 156:** *left*, courtesy of Moen **Page 158:** Dreamstime **Page 159:** *top left and right*, courtesy of Smith + Noble; *bottom*, courtesy of American Bath Factory **Page 160:** *all*, courtesy of Kohler **Page 162:** *bottom right*, courtesy of Velux America, Inc. **Pages 166–67:** courtesy of Delta Faucet Company **Page 168:** courtesy of Delta Faucet Company **Page 169:** *top*, courtesy of Villeroy & Boch; *bottom*, courtesy of Kohler **Page 170:** *top*, courtesy of Tech Lighting; *bottom*, courtesy of Delta Faucet Company **Page 171:** *top*, courtesy of Tech Light-ing; *bottom left*, courtesy of LBL Lighting; *bottom right*, courtesy of Delta Faucet Company **Page 172:** courtesy of LBL Lighting **Pages 173–75:** *all*, Dave Toht and Rebecca Anderson **Page 176:** *left*, courtesy of Tech Lighting **Page 178:** Freeze Frame/CH **Pages 180–81:** *all*, Freeze Frame/CH **Pages 182–83:** *all*, Freeze Frame/CH **Page 184:** courtesy of iapsales.com LLC **Page 185:** *top left and inset*, Freeze Frame/CH; *top right and bottom three plus inset*, Brian Nieves/CH **Page 189:** *right*, courtesy of Mr. Steam **Pages 190–91:** courtesy of Armstrong **Page 192:** courtesy of Dal-Tile **Page 193:** *top left*, courtesy of Walker Zanger; *top right*, courtesy of Kohler; *bottom*, courtesy of Dal-Tile **Page 194:** *all*, courtesy of Dal-Tile **Page 195:** *top*, courtesy of Armstrong; *bottom*, courtesy of Hakatai Enterprises **Page 197:** *top left and right*, Freeze Frame/CH; *bottom*, courtesy of Dal-Tile **Page 198:** *all*, John Parsekian/CH **Page 199:** *top left and right*, Freeze Frame/CH **Page 200:** courtesy of Dal-Tile **Page 206:** *top*, courtesy of Dal-Tile; *bottom*, courtesy of Kohler **Page 209:** *top left and right*, courtesy of Dal-Tile **Page 210:** *left*, courtesy of Armstrong; *top and bottom right*, Freeze Frame/CH **Pages 212–13:** Merle Henkenius/CH **Pages 214–17:** *all*, Brian Nieves/CH **Pages 218–19:** *all*, Freeze Frame **Pages 220–25:** *all*, Merle Henkenius **Page 232:** courtesy of Dal-Tile **Page 235:** courtesy of Kohler **Pages 236–37:** *all*, courtesy of American Olean

Metric Equivalents

Length

1 inch	25.4mm
1 foot	0.3048m
1 yard	0.9144m
1 mile	1.61km

Area

1 square inch	645mm^2
1 square foot	0.0929m^2
1 square yard	0.8361m^2
1 acre	4046.86m^2
1 square mile	2.59km^2

Volume

1 cubic inch	16.3870cm^3
1 cubic foot	0.03m^3
1 cubic yard	0.77m^3

Common Lumber Equivalents

Sizes: Metric cross sections are so close to their U.S. sizes, as noted below, that for most purposes they may be considered equivalents.

Dimensional lumber	1 x 2	19 x 38mm
	1 x 4	19 x 89mm
	2 x 2	38 x 38mm
	2 x 4	38 x 89mm
	2 x 6	38 x 140mm
	2 x 8	38 x 184mm
	2 x 10	38 x 235mm
	2 x 12	38 x 286mm
Sheet sizes	4 x 8 ft.	1200 x 2400mm
	4 x 10 ft.	1200 x 3000mm
Sheet thickness	1/4 in.	6mm
	3/8 in.	9mm
	1/2 in.	12mm
	3/4 in.	19mm
Stud/joist spacing	16 in. o.c.	400mm o.c.
	24 in. o.c.	600mm o.c.

Capacity

1 fluid ounce	29.57mL
1 pint	473.18mL
1 quart	0.95L
1 gallon	3.79L

Weight

1 ounce	28.35g
1 pound	0.45kg

Temperature

Fahrenheit = Celsius x 1.8 + 32
Celsius = Fahrenheit - 32 x 5/9

Nail Size and Length

Penny Size	Nail Length
2d	1"
3d	1¼"
4d	1½"
5d	1¾"
6d	2"
7d	2¼"
8d	2½"
9d	2¾"
10d	3"
12d	3¼"
16d	3½"

Have a home improvement, decorating, or gardening project? Look for these and other fine Creative Homeowner books wherever books are sold.

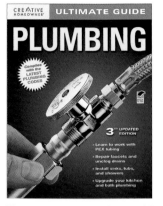

The complete manual for plumbing projects. Over 775 color photos and illustrations. 304 pp.; 8¹/₂" × 10⁷/₈"
BOOK #: CH278205

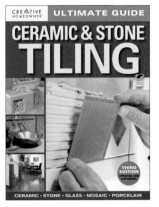

Complete DIY tile instruction. Over 550 color photos and illustrations. 240 pp.; 8¹/₂" × 10⁷/₈"
BOOK #: CH277525

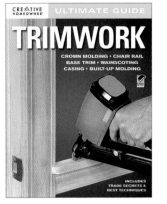

Transform a room with trimwork. Over 975 photos and illustrations. 288 pp.; 8¹/₂" × 10⁷/₈"
BOOK #: CH277511

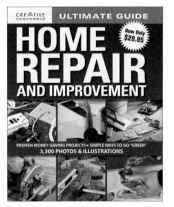

The ultimate home-improvement reference manual. Over 300 step-by-step projects. 608 pp.; 9¹/₄" × 10⁷/₈"
BOOK #: CH267880

Complete source book for molding trim. Over 1,000 color photos and illos. 256 pp.; 8¹/₂" × 10⁷/₈"
BOOK #: CH279402

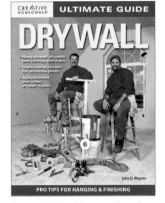

A complete guide, covering all aspects of drywall. Over 380 color photos. 176 pp.; 8¹/₂" × 10⁷/₈"
BOOK #: CH278330

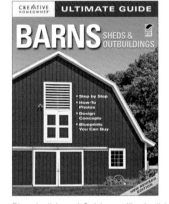

Plan, build, and finish a utility building. Over 975 color photos and illustrations. 288 pp.; 8¹/₂" × 10⁷/₈"
BOOK #: CH277815

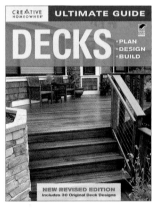

Information to design and build a deck or patio. Over 900 photos and illos. 368 pp.; 8¹/₂" × 10⁷/₈"
BOOK #: CH277170

Inspiration for creating an attractive, up-to-date kitchen. Over 500 color photos. 224 pp.; 8¹/₂" × 10⁷/₈"
BOOK #: CH279412

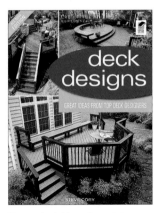

Great deck ideas from top designers. Over 450 color photos. 240 pp.; 8¹/₂" × 10⁷/₈"
BOOK #: CH277382

The quick and easy way to grow fruit and vegetables. Over 300 color photos and illos. 224 pp.; 8¹/₂" × 10⁷/₈"
BOOK #: CH274557

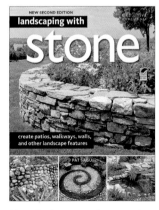

Ideas for incorporating stone into the landscape. Over 335 color photos. 224 pp.; 8¹/₂" × 10⁷/₈"
BOOK #: CH274179

For more information and to order direct, visit our Web site at **www.creativehomeowner.com**